WASTE
INCINERATION
Pocket Hand Book

By
Paul Cheremisinoff, P.E.

FOREWORD

It is estimated that industry spends \$ 5 - billion to treat hazardous wastes and that amount is expected to double by 1990, when U.S. plants will be treating some 280 million metric tons per year of waste. Pressures are growing for alternatives to landfills for all types of wastes handling. The costs of placing wastes in landfills has doubled since 1984 and increasingly stringent regulations and restrictions as well as environmental impacts and concerns will make the practice more difficult.

Destruction and detoxification of wastes include a broad range of widely varying processes. **Incineration** is often identified as the ultimate in practical destruction and certainly affords a most effective form of managing disposal of many wastes, such as combustible solids, semisolids, suldges, concentrated liquid wastes and gases. It reduces, if not eliminates, potential environmental risks and often can potentially convert wastes into recoverable energy. Comparing incineration to other disposal options, advantages become evident in specific applications, especially as more wastes become regulated and as added prohibitions and increasingly burdensome costs are placed on land disposal.

This book intends to provide a pocket guide to waste incineration for the pollution control engineer and manager. Included are basic concepts and data on wastes combustion, and an overview of process technologies in the market place. It should assist in the incineration decision making process and a basis for those who wish to dig deeper.

This small book is affectionately dedicated to **Louise** who in no small way made it possible and is lovingly remembered. A final note of thanks to **Dick Young** of **Pollution Engineering** magazine and **Pudvan Publishing Co.** for their charge and encouragement in producing this volume.

Paul **N.** Cheremisinoff

About the author

Paul N. Cheremisinoff - is Professor of Civil and Environmental Engineering, Director of the Physical Treatment Div., of the NSF Industry/University Cooperative Center for Research for Hazardous & Toxic Substances and Director of the Center for Training for Hazardous Occupations & Environments at **New Jersey Institute of Technology.** Prof. Cheremisinoff has more than 40 - years experience in research, design, consulting for a wide range of government industry organizations. He is author and coauthor of numerous papers and books on environment, energy, biotechnology, computers and electro-technology and is a licenced professional engineer, Fellow of the New York Academy of Sciences and a member of Sigma Xi and Tau Beta Pi.

CONTENTS

WASTES INCINERATION
POCKET HANDBOOK

COMBUSTION PRINCIPLES

Incineration can be defined as a unit operation that employs thermal decomposition via oxidation to reduce carbonaceous matter. The principal products of incineration are carbon-dioxide, water, ash, and waste heat. In addition, various by-products having environmental importance are generated, such as sulfur and nitrogen compounds, halogens, and various heavy metals (e.g., lead, cadmium, mercury, and others).

Typical industrial incinerators are integrated systems composed of the incinerator, raw waste and auxiliary material handling equipment, exhaust gas cleaning devices, effluent liquid treatment, solids discharge control, and energy and by-product recovery operations.

Principles

The principal products of combustion are carbon dioxide, water, sulfur dioxide, and nitrogen. These generally are in the most highly oxidized state that is stable for each element of the fuel. This definition of complete combustion is somewhat arbitrary. Some nitrogen is converted to oxides, in particular nitric oxide. Sulfur, if present, is also converted to its oxidized state. Metals such as iron and aluminum may also be converted to oxides; chlorine if present to HCl.

In the application of incineration, combustion is a high-temperature process. Heat released by combustion is partly stored in the combustion products and partly transferred by conduction, convection, and radiation both to incinerator walls and to the incoming fuel is required for ignition.

Incineration should be designed around the three "Ts" of combustion, namely, **time, temperature and turbulence** in the presence of oxygen. Systems that do not embrace these factors in their design, experience operating and maintenance problems as well as pose environmental hazards.

Time is accounted for in design through the space and volume of the combustion chambers of the incinerator. Volume must be sufficient to retain the gas flow long enough to allow complete combustion of fuel or solid wastes and volatile gases.

Temperature is a critical consideration. Heat is the driving force to sustain combustion, and in many instances supplemental heat must be supplied by auxiliary burners to preheat the incinerators or to support combustion of materials having high moisture levels and low heating values.

System hydrodynamics plays a major role in combustion efficiency. **Turbulence** can be designed into the incinerator by a series of baffles or constrictions. The purpose of turbulence is to promote mixing between the products of combustion and air (oxygen). Oxygen is provided to complete the combustion process. in the case of small refuse incinerators, application is aimed at the burning of cellulose (1 lb of cellulose releases approximately 8,000 Btu's of heat). In this reaction, cellulose combines with oxygen to form CO_2 and H_2O. Municipal incinerators are designed on the basis of 4,500 to 5,000 Btu/lb of refuse burned because the heterogeneity of mixed refuse properties and moisture present.

Fuel-to-Air Ratio

A basic requirement for efficient combustion is that fuel (waste) and air be mixed in proper proportions and under conditions that prompt ignition and maintain combustion. For gaseous, liquid, or pulverized solid fuels this criteria is readily met; however, with solid refuse and some waste the variability of physical and chemical properties often makes this a difficult condition to meet. Because of this variability and the prevalence of such material as glass and metals, combustion is generally carried out in deep fuel beds for solids (e.g., municipal wastes).

We may consider an idealized system, such as a bed of double-screened coke. Depending on the relative movement of air and fuel and the resultant flow of heat and combustion materials, fuel beds may be classified as follows:

3

- Underfeed beds in which fuel and air flow in the same direction.

- Overfeed beds in which fuel and air flow in the opposite direction.

- Crossfeed beds in which fuel and air flow in directions at some angle to each other so that the heat required for ignition neither flows directly against the air stream not directly with the initial combustion products.

The underfeed bed arrangement is illustrated in Figure 1-1A. The flow of heat against the air stream produces a sharp temperature gradient at a level over the raw face designated as the ignition plane. Oxygen is rapidly consumed by the reaction:

$$O_2 + C \quad \longrightarrow \quad CO_2 \tag{1}$$

as the gases move through the ignition plane and into the ignited fuel. As the oxygen is depleted the reaction becomes:

$$CO_2 + C \quad \longrightarrow \quad 2\ CO \tag{2}$$

Reaction 2 shows that the CO_2 concentration decreases, producing carbon monoxide. The reaction absorbs heat so that the temperature fails as the gases flow toward the ash layer above the ignited fuel. The relative distribution of temperature and concentration of combustion products is shown in Figure 1-1B.

In the overfeed fuel bed (Figure 1-2A), the incoming air passes first through the ash layers, heat recuperation favors higher temperatures, and greater and more rapid conversion of CO_2

to CO takes place. The relative distribution of combustion products and temperature are shown in Figure 1-2B.

Figure 1-3 shows the crossfeed fuel bed where gas flow is from the raw fuel into the ignited fuel but heat flow for ignition does not flow directly against the gas stream. The relative direction of fuel and velocities are important in the fuel bed classification. Batch burning in a pot with top ignition and air feed from the bottom is referred to as underfeed burning even though there is no fuel flow. Similarly bottom ignition with airfeed from the bottom would be overfeed burning. Horizontal fuel flow with airfeed from the bottom, as on a moving grate, and corresponding to a 90° rotation of Figure 1-3 would be crossfeed burning.

The role of ignition may be measured in terms of the rate of advance of the ignition plane into the raw fuel. The plane of ignition can be defined as the plane within the fuel bed beyond which there is a sharp temperature gradient from that of the raw fuel to that of fully ignited fuel.

The management of fuel and air can take many forms. Good management can be illustrated best by summarizing conditions that lead to good composition in deep fuel beds. These are as follows:

- Raw fuel should be fed in such a manner as to provide underfeed or crossfeed burning. Large masses of raw fuel

5

should never be dumped directly on top of the flames.

- As in underfeed and crossfeed burning, gas flow should be from raw fuel into ignited fuel.

- Overfire air must be mixed with the hot gases flowing out of the fuel bed. This is best accomplished by such devices as overfire-air jets to give turbulent mixing close to the intense-burning zone. That is, streams of gas from colder portions of the fuel bed must be directed into zones of intense burning.

- Additional mixing with high amounts of excess air that may be desired to give lower gas temperatures must be delayed so as not to hinder good combustion.

More novel modes of fuel / air management are used in vortex and fluidized - bed combustion. In vortex combustion all of the air can be supplied as overfire air. The aerodynamics of the vortex is such that the air must follow a downward spiral to scrub the fuel bed and mix with rising volatile matter. In fluidized-bed combustion, waste is fed into a turbulent bed of granular inert material. Through proper balance between heat input in fuel, heat losses to the surroundings, heat extraction from the bed and enthalpy of combustion products leaving the bed, the temperature can be maintained at a level that provides good combustion. The temperature also is practically constant throughout a well-fluidized bed. Good heat transfer between hot granu-

6

lar material and incoming solid fuel causes prompt devolatiliza-
tion and ignition.

Material and Thermal Balances

Considering the more complex application of solid waste
incineration. Table 1-1 and 1-2 provide general information and
typical compositions of refuse. Since temperature, as well as
the degree of contacting between fuel and air, is important to
the combustion process, the effect of refuse composition on the
air requirements, and the effect of excess air on the gas temperature produced must be examined. Information for the analysis
of air, and the ultimate analysis and gross heating value of the
refuse is first required.

The composition of air is approximately constant, except for
its moisture content. The assumed composition on a basis of 70%
relative humidity at 60° F is given in the footnote b of Table 1-
3. Note that refuse composition varies considerably, depending
on such factors as source (domestic, commercial, etc.), geograp-
hy, and climatic conditions.

Material balances are performed on the basis of atomic
weights units of the fuel elements and the moles of combustion
products. This is necessary simplification since each atomic
weight unit contains the same number of atoms; and each volume of
gas, under standard conditions of temperature and pressure, occu-

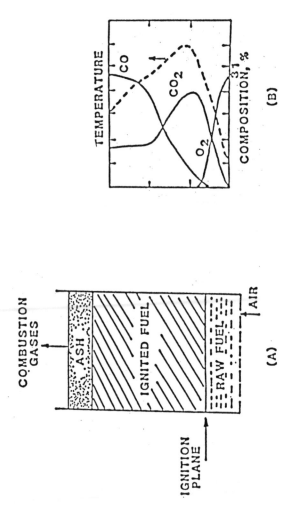

Figure]-]. (A) Shows idealized underfeed fuel bed; (B) plot of relative distribution of temperature and combustion products.

8

TABLE 1-1.

Classification of Refuse Materials

Refuse (Solid Wastes)	Composition		Source
Garbage	Wastes from the preparation, cooking, and serving of food Market refuse, waste from the handling, storage, and sale of produce and meat		Households, institutions, and commercial concerns such as hotels, stores, restaurants, markets, etc.
Rubbish	Combustible (primarily organic)	Paper, cardboard, cartons Wood, boxes, excelsior Plastics Rags, cloth, bedding Leather, rubber Grass, leaves, yard trimmings Metals, tin cans, metal foils Dirt	
	Noncombustible (primarily inorganic)	Stones, bricks, ceramics, crockery Glass, bottles Other mineral refuse	
Ashes	Residue from fires used for cooking and for heating buildings, cinders		
Bulky wastes	Large auto parts, tires Stoves, refrigerators, other large appliances Furniture, large crates Trees, branches, palm fronds, stumps, flotage		
Street refuse	Street sweepings, dirt Leaves Catch-basin dirt Contents of litter receptacles		Streets, sidewalks, alleys, vacant lots, etc.
Dead animals	Small animals: cats, dogs, poultry, etc. Large animals: horses, cows, etc.		
Abandoned vehicles	Automobiles, trucks		
Construction and demolition wastes	Lumber, roofing, and sheathing scraps Rubble, broken concrete, plaster, etc. Conduit, pipe, wire, insulation, etc.		
Industrial refuse	Solid wastes resulting from industrial processes and manufacturing operations, such as food-processing wastes, boiler house cinders, wood, plastic, and metal scraps and shavings, etc.		Factories, power plants, etc.
Special wastes	Hazardous wastes: pathological wastes, explosives, radioactive materials Security wastes: confidential documents, negotiable papers, etc.		Households, hospitals, institutions, stores, industry, etc.
Animal and agricultural wastes	Manures, crop residues		Farms, feed lots
Sewage-treatment residues	Coarse screenings, grit, septic-tank sludge, dewatered sludge		Sewage-treatment plants, septic tanks

From American Public Works Association

9

Table 1-2.
Composition and Analysis of an Average Municipal Refuse
(Studies Made by Purdue University)

Component	Percent of All Refuse by Weight	Moisture (percent by weight)	Volatile Matter	Analysis (percent dry weight)					Non-combustibles	Caloric Value (Btu/lb)
				Carbon	Hydrogen	Oxygen	Nitrogen	Sulfur		
Rubbish, 64%										
Paper	42.0	10.2	84.6	43.4	5.8	44.3	0.3	0.20	6.0	7,572
Wood	2.4	20.0	84.9	50.5	6.0	42.4	0.2	0.05	1.0	8,613
Grass	4.0	65.0	—	43.3	6.0	41.7	2.2	0.05	6.8	7,693
Brush	1.5	40.0	—	42.5	5.9	41.2	2.0	0.05	8.3	7,900
Greens	1.5	62.0	70.3	40.3	5.6	39.0	2.0	0.05	13.0	7,077
Leaves	5.0	50.0	—	40.5	6.0	45.1	0.2	0.05	8.2	7,096
Leather	0.3	10.0	76.2	60.0	8.0	11.5	10.0	0.40	10.1	8,850
Rubber	0.6	1.2	85.0	77.7	10.4	—	—	2.0	10.0	11,330
Plastics	0.7	2.0	—	60.0	7.2	22.6	—	—	10.2	14,368
Oils, paints	0.8	0.0	—	66.9	9.7	5.2	2.0	—	16.3	13,400
Linoleum	0.1	2.1	65.8	48.1	5.3	18.7	0.1	0.40	27.4	8,310
Rags	0.6	10.0	93.6	55.0	6.6	31.2	4.6	0.13	2.5	7,652
Street sweepings	3.0	20.0	67.4	34.7	4.8	35.2	0.1	0.20	25.0	6,000
Dirt	1.0	3.2	21.2	20.6	2.6	4.0	0.5	0.01	72.3	3,790
Unclassified	0.5	4.0	—	16.6	2.5	18.4	0.05	0.05	62.5	3,000
Food Wastes, 12%										
Garbage	10.0	72.0	53.3	45.0	6.4	28.8	3.3	0.52	16.0	8,484
Fats	2.0	0.0	—	76.7	12.1	11.2	0	0	0	16,700
Noncombustibles, 24%										
Metals	8.0	3.0	0.5	0.8	0.04	0.2	—	—	99.0	124
Glass and ceramics	6.0	2.0	0.4	0.6	0.03	0.1	—	—	99.3	65
Ashes	10.0	10.0	3.0	28.0	0.5	0.8	—	0.5	70.2	4,172
Composite Refuse, as Received										
All refuse	100	20.7	—	28.0	3.5	22.4	0.33	0.16	24.9	6,203

From American Public Works Association [1].

pies the same volume. In other words, ideal conditions of temperature and pressure, occupies the same volume. In other words,
ideal gas behavior is assumed, which is a good approximation
within the practical limits for air under atmospheric conditions
as well as for combustion gases. The exception to this is when
the moisture condensate is high at temperatures below the dew-
point. However, within these limits the gas composition in terms
of percent by volume are the same as the mole percents.

The second column of Table 1-3 provides the weight percent
in the particular refuse for each element as identified in the
first column. Using a 100 lb refuse basis, the weight percents
then correspond to pounds of each element. Division by the
atomic weight gives the atomic-weight units (fourth column) for
each element. Each atomic weight unit of carbon requires 1 mole
of oxygen to produce 1 mole of CO_2. These quantities are shown
in the fifth and seventh columns of Table 1-3. An atomic-weight
unit of hydrogen requires 1/4 mole of oxygen to produce 1/2 mole
of water. Each atomic weight unit of oxygen in refuse represents
a 1/2 mole of oxygen that need not be supplied by air to form
combustion products. It is assumed that the nitrogen of the
refuse forms N_2 in the combustion products. This calculation
ignores small percentage of nitrogen oxide that are typically
found in combustion gases. The error is negligible in comparison
to the percentages of other products. Thus each atomic weight

unit produces 1/2mole of N_2. Like the carbon, each atomic weight unit ofsulfur requires a mole of O_2 to produce a mole of SO_2. Since the sulfur percentages are low and only a few percent of the SO_2 is oxidized to SO_3, the moles of SO_3 and the extra oxygen required for its formation can be neglected in determining gas composition and the oxygen requirement.

The total oxygen requirement, 2.727 moles, includes a negative item corresponding to oxygen in the refuse. The air required at zero excess, 13.18 moles per 100 lb. of refuse, is determined by dividing the oxygen requirement by its volume (or mole) fraction in air as shown at the bottom of Table 1-3.

The weight per mole of a mixed gas is calculated as the sum of volume fractions times its molecular weights. Thus, for air of the assumed composition (note b, Table 1-3)

$0.0003(44.011)+0.7802(28.016)+0.2069(32)+0.0126(18.016)=28.7$ lb/mole.

It now is apparent that 3.78 lb air are required per lb of refuse. The moles of combustion product derived from the air are found by multiplying the moles of air required by the volume fractions in air of CO_2, H_2O, and N_2. All the oxygen of the air, at zero excess, is included in the combustion product of the refuse. Since the percent by volume is practically equal to the mole percent, the composition of the product gas is obtained from the total moles for each gas as a percentage of the grand total.

12

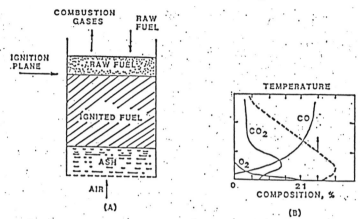

Figure]-2. (A) Shows idealized overfeed fuel bed; (B) plot of relative distribution of temperature and combustion products.

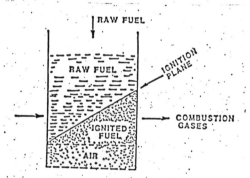

.Figure]-3. Shows idealized crossfeed fuel bed.

Table 1-3.

Calculation of Air Requirement and Gas Composition at Zero Excess Air

Component	Weight Percent	Atomic Weight	Atomic Weight Units	Moles of Oxygen Required	Combustion Product	Moles of Combustion Products			
						From Combustion	From Air	Total	Percent
Carbon	29.83	12.011	2.484	2.484	Carbon dioxide	2.484	0.004	2.488	15.5
Hydrogen	6.23	1.008	6.181	1.545	Water	3.090	0.166	3.256	20.3
Oxygen	43.45	16.000	2.716	-1.358	—	—	—	—	—
Nitrogen	0.37	14.008	0.026	—	Nitrogen	0.013	10.283	10.296	64.2
Sulfur	0.12	32.066	0.004	0.004	Sulfur dioxide	0.004	—	0.004	00.02
Ash and metal	20.0	—	—	0.052	—	—	—	—	—
Total	100.00			2.727				16.044	100.0

Moles of air required per 100 lb fuel = 2.727/.2069 = 13.18
Pounds of air required per pound of refuse = 13.18(28.7)/100 = 3.78
Moles of air per mole of gas = 13.18/16.044 = 0.8215
Moles of gas produced per pounds of refuse = 16.044/100 = 0.16044

a Computation is based on 100 lbs of refuse.
b Assumed air composition, in volume fractions: carbon dioxide, 0.0003; nitrogen, 0.7803; oxygen, 0.2093; water, 0.0126, assuming ideal gases, the volume fractions may be taken as mole fractions and are equal to the percentages by volume divided by 100. The composition as given is for rare gases included with the nitrogen and with moisture content corresponding to 70% relative humidity at 60 F. Air of this composition has a weight of 28.7 lb per mole of total gas.
c Per 100 lb of refuse.
d 13.18(0.0126) = 0.166, for balance.
e Includes hydrogen and oxygen from 20% moisture.
f An assumed value for partial burning of metals.
From Ornberg

14

The calculation of gas composition at various excess air levels is illustrated in Table 1-4. The composition is based on 100 moles of combustion products at zero excess air. Total moles per 100 moles of combustion products at zero excess air are given in column 3 for each excess air level. This will be used later for the thermal balance calculation. The gas composition is given on a moist basis. An approximate calculation of the theoretical air requirements can be based on the heating value of refuse or wastes and generally that appears in the fuel. Table 1-5 gives the pounds of air requirement for releasing 1,000 Btu for complete combustion of the given fuel for a series of organic compounds containing carbon, hydrogen, and oxygen.

Figure 1-4 shows the air requirement as a function of refuse heating value. The plot is based on an air requirement of 0.7 lb/1,000 Btu of heat released. If the gross heating value of the refuse is known, the amount of air required per pound of refuse can be obtained directly from the plot for various excess air levels.

A modified Dulong formula is sometimes useful in estimating the gross heating value from the fuel analysis;

$$\text{gross Btu/lb} = 145.4C + 620\left(H - \frac{O}{8}\right) + 41S \tag{3}$$

where C, H, O, and S are the weight percentages of carbon, hydrogen, oxygen, and sulfur. The term (H - O/8) represents hydrogen

Table I-4.
Effect of Excess Air on Gas Composition

Percent Excess Air[a]	Moles Excess Air[c]	Total Moles	Gas Composition[b]				
			CO_2	O_2	N_2	H_2O	SO_2
0	0.00	100.00	15.50	0.00	64.20	20.30	0.02
			15.50	0.00	64.20	20.30	0.02
50	[d]41.08	141.08	15.51	8.50	96.23	[e]20.82	0.02
			11.0	6.0	68.2	14.8	0.01
125	102.69	202.69	15.53	21.24	144.31	21.59	0.02
			7.7	10.5	71.2	10.6	0.01

a *Based on 100 moles of gas at zero excess air.*
b *Composition is given in moles in the first line and in percent in the second line.*

c *Percent of excess air* $= \dfrac{100 \ (air \ supplied - theoretical \ air \ requirement)}{theoretical \ air \ requirement}$

d *Excess-air requirement is calculated from the ratio of the theoretical air requirement to gas produced (from Table 2-1) as*

$\left(\dfrac{moles \ of \ air}{moles \ of \ gas}\right)$ *(percent of excess air)* $= 0.8215(50) = 41.08$

moles of excess air per 100 moles of gas produced at zero excess air.
e *Calculation of the moles of product gas is illustrated for water at 50% excess air as (moles excess air)*
$\left(\dfrac{moles \ of \ water}{moles \ of \ air}\right)$ *+ (moles of water per 100 moles of product gas at zero excess air)* =
$41.08(0.0126) \times 20.30 = 20.82.$
From Baillie, Donner, and Galli

Table I-5.
Air Requirement per 1,000 Btu for Various Compounds

Compounds	Pounds of air per 1,000 Btu
Methane	0.73
Methyl alcohol	0.67
Propane	0.73
Propylene	0.71
Benzene	0.74
Glucose	0.69
Glycol dipalmitate	0.74
Cellulose	0.68

From Baillie

16

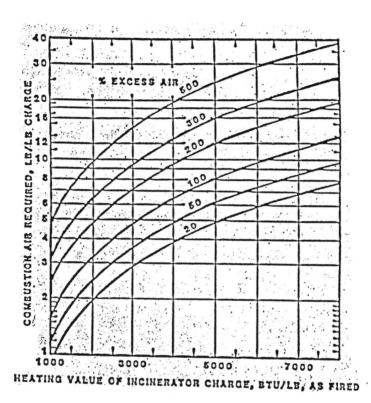

Figure]-4. Plot of air requirement vs. heating value for refuse.
Source: Balie

in the fuel that is combined with oxygen as moisture as well as hydrogen and oxygen that are combined with the fuel in some other form. An approximate calculation of the excess air can be obtained from the product gas analysis expressed in percent by volume. The excess air is given as:

$$\% \text{ of excess air} = \frac{100 \ (O_2)}{(20.69/78.02)(N_2) - O_2} \qquad (4)$$

The denominator of this expression represents the oxygen requirement and is expressed as the difference between the oxygen equivalent to the nitrogen supplied and the oxygen remaining. Multiplying the ratio of oxygen remaining by the oxygen supplied provides the percent of excess air. Note that this computation is approximate because sulfur and nitrogen contents of the fuel are assumed.

Sulfur dioxide is included with CO_2 in the gas analysis. This involves the same oxygen consumption per mole. Error due to the approximation of the content is limited by the small retention of sulfur in the ash and by the small conversion to sulfur trioxide instead of the dioxide. Error due to nitrogen in the fuel is also small because of the relatively large portion of N_2 supplied by the air. Error in the present illustration is less than that due to the limited precision of the actual gas analysis. These errors may magnify with materials that are high in nitrogen content, such as proteins.

We now direct attention to the thermal balance. The enthalpy for a given amount of gas is the heat needed at constant pressure to raise the temperature from a standard state to some required level. A computation of the temperature of the product gas, with an assumed percentage of the ehat derived from the fuel remaining in the product gas is needed. One approach is to perform such a calculation for an arbitrarily chosen fuel synthesis, however, for general purposes, it is more convenient to perform computations in an opposite direction. The enthalpy of that amount of product gas corresponding to 1 lb of a given fuel is calculated for a variety of excess air levels and temperatures. Comparison of these values to the percentage of the heating value of the fuel that may be assumed to remain in the product gas gives an estimate of the gas temperature.

Data required for this computation are given in Table 1-6. The enthalpy of the gas at a given temperature and excess-air level can be determined from the following relation.

$$
\left(\frac{\text{theoretical moles of product gas}}{\text{pound of refuse}}\right) \left(\frac{\text{total moles of gas}}{\text{theoretical moles of gas}}\right)
$$

[Summation of (mole fraction of gas Component) Btu per mole of gas component]

$$
= \frac{\text{Btu in product gas}}{\text{pounds of refuse}} \tag{5}
$$

19

Table I-6
Enthalpies
(Btu per Pound Mole over Standard State*)

Temperature T (°F)	CO_2	O_2	N_2	H_2O
1,000	10,048	6,974	6,720	26,925
1,500	16,214	11,008	10,556	31,743
2,000	22,719	15,191	14,520	36,903
2,500	29,539	19,517	18,609	42,405

Enthalpy Equations

$$CO_2 \quad H = 10,570\left(\frac{T+460}{1,000}\right) + 583.3\left(\frac{T+460}{1,000}\right)^2 + \frac{667.4}{(T+460)/1,000} - 7,085$$

$$O_2 \quad H = 7,160\left(\frac{T+460}{1,000}\right) + 278.8\left(\frac{T+460}{1,000}\right)^2 + \frac{129.6}{(T+460)/1,000} - 4,163$$

$$N_2 \quad H = 6,830\left(\frac{T+460}{1,000}\right) + 250.0\left(\frac{T+460}{1,000}\right)^2 + \frac{38.9}{(T+460)/1,000} - 3,811$$

$$H_2O \quad H = 7,300\left(\frac{T+460}{1,000}\right) + 683.3\left(\frac{T+460}{1,000}\right)^2 + 14,810$$

* Gas, except liquid water, at 1 atm pressure and 77° F.
From Bailie

Table I-7
Heat Content of Combustion Product Gases

Temperature (°F)	Heat Content of Gas from 1 lb of Refuse (Btu)	
	50% Excess Air	125% Excess Air
1,000	2,284	2,973
1,500	3,246	4,320
2,000	4,250	5,721
2,500	5,294	7,176

From Bailie

20

Illustrative data for such a calculation are given in Table 1-3, 1-4, and 1-6. Mole fractions are equal to the percentages divided by 100. As an example, for 50% excess air and 1,500° F the result is:

$$0.16044\left(\frac{141.08}{100}\right)[0.110(16,214)+0.060(11,008)+0.682(10,556)+0.148$$
$$(31,743)]$$

= 3246 Btu/pound of refuse.

Data for two excess air levels and for four temperatures are given in Table 1-7. The gross heating value of the refuse in this example is 5,442 (Btu/lb). This heat must be distributed between the product gas and ash residues or be lost through the incinerator walls. If the loss through the walls and in ash residues are assumed to be 10% of the total, 4,898 Btu/lb of refuse must remain in the gas. An interpolation between the data of Table 1-7 indicates that the gas temperature should be about 2,300° F at 50% excess air or 1,700° F at 125% excess air.

Combustion Calculations

Combustion of refuse or wastes involves the usual parameters but in a more complex manner because of te heterogeneous nature of the fuel. The most difficult factors to be accomodated are the amounts of moisture and the noncombustibles in wastes. The average heat content of waste is actually consistent, but from

21

instant to instant, the heat content can vary substantially. This implies that a degree of premixing is required to insure that a minimum of moisture and maximum of combustibles are available to the process and that the resulting mixture is capable of supporting combustion, otherwise supplemental fuel is required.

Once mixing has been accomplished, the material must be dried and raised to the ignition temperature. At this point, air must be available in sufficient quantity to support combustion. The air and refuse must be mixed in a turbulent manner. This operation takes time, which means that certain furnace velocities and volumes are required to properly complete the process and release the heat available in the refuse, waste.

Drying is accomplished by convective and radiant heat transfer mechanixms. Convective transfer is derived from the air or gas flows, whereas radiant transfer occurs from the flames over furnace surface. The material can be either predried external to the furnace or dried within the unit itself as a consequence of the burning system's design.

Predrying can be accomplished in several ways, including flash drying, drying in rotary drums, trays, chute or fluid bed dryers. External drying can be accomplished with gases drawn from the furnace or incinerator exit. These gases must be returned and reheated for deodorizing purposes. Drying can be done

with preheated air from a gas to an air heat exchanger in accomplished with air, it must enter into the combustion process or
the odors produced will have to be taken care of separately.
Without mixing, the load on the drying system will be erratic.

A furnace can be desinged so that drying is accomplished
within the enclosure itself. Most modern incinerators incorporate furnace drying rateher than predrying ahead of the furnace.
An exception is where one, is attempting to burn material such as
sewage or industrial sludges. The specific application will
dictate the system design choice.

If the drying is external to the surface, the refuse is
brought to about 220° F and the rest of the sensible heat addition required to bring the refuse to ignition temperature is
added to the furnace. This requires an additional 1,200 Btu/lb
to be added to the refuse in the external predrying system to
evaporate residual moisture.

This 1,200 Btu was arrived at by comparing with the requirements for evaporating a pound of water and some of the factors
that affect drying. It requires 1,122.3 Btu to evaporate 1 lb of
water from a mass of refuse at an ambient tempereature of 60° F.
Since drying equipment is not 100% thermally effective, the heat
input to accomplish the required evaporation must be greater.
The effectiveness of a thermal drying process is governed by four
fundamental factors:

23

- Moisture dispersion within the waste - refuse mass, allowing maximum exposure of moisture surfaces to the heated gas.
- Large temperature differentials - high gas temperatures are required for rapid drying (i.e., a high rate of heat transfer).
- Maximum refuse agitation to increase the rate of heat transfer.
- Particle sizes must be at a minimum to increase the surface from which moisture can be evaporated and allow the moisture to reach the surface for drying in the case of solids.

This last requirement coupled with the fact that oxidation as well as evaporation are surface pehnomena, indicates that a decrease in particle size of the refuse will improve not only its drying, but its combustion, once in the furnace. This argues for some form of preparation if maximum efficiency is to be obtained in both the drying and burning operations.

Internal drying, if the furnace is of the mass burning type, is usually accomplished on a stoker, the first grate system of which must dry and ignite the refuse. This is accomplished by designing the furnace so that the drying stoker is gas swept and exposed to the high-temperature furnace surfaces. This enables convective and radiant drying to be accomplished rapidly.

Once the mixed refuse has been dried, sensible heat from the furnace flame and enclosure must be added to bring the material to its ignition temperature and begin the rapid oxidation known as combustion, releasing the heat contained in the refuse waste fuel.

Burning With Sufficient Air

Although refuse appears highly variable, typical refuse is quite uniform in chemical analysis and fits into a family tree fossil fuels as shown in Figure 1-5. Both industrial and municipal refuse bear close relation to wood, bark, and bagasse. Typical heating values of various wastes are listed in Table 1-8.

The variables in refuse are mostly the noncombustible residues and moisture, whereas the chemical composition of combustibles is uniform. Tests have shown that the heat of combustion on a moisture ash-free basis is very close to that of cellulose (8,000 Btu/lb for normal municipal and most industrial refuse fuel). This fact simplifies the calculations in the heat process and makes it possible to predict the behavior of the burning material. The most important variable is moisture in the refuse, which is considered one of the main energy-consuming loads on the incinerator.

The heating values of the main constituents of municipal and industrial refuse on a moisture and ash-free basis are:

Table I-8.
Refuse Heating Value

Type Refuse	Moisture (%)	BTU as fired
Domestic Refuse		
Paper, cardboard, cartons, bags	3	7,660
Wood crates, boxes, scrap	7	7,825
Brush, branches	17	7,140
Leaves	30	4,900
Grass	50	3,820
Garbage	75	1,820
Greenstuff	50	3,470
Greens	50	4,070
Rags, cotton, linen	10	6,440
Industrial Scrap Refuse		
Boot, shoe trim and scrap		8,500
Sponge waffle and scrap		8,500
Butyl soles scrap		11,500
Cement wet scrap		11,500
Rubber		12,420
Tire cord scrap		12,400
Rubber scorched scrap		19,700
Tires, bus and auto		18,000
Gum scrap		19,700
Latex coagulum		19,700
Latex waste, coagulum waste		12,000
Leather scrap		10,000
Waxed paper		12,000
Cork scrap		12,400
Paraffin		16,803
Oil waste, fuel oil residue		18,000
Plastic and Synthetic Refuse		
Cellophane plastic		12,000
Polyethylene		19,840
Polyvinyl chloride		17,500
Vinyl scrap		17,500
Aldehyde sludge		18,150
Solvent naptha		18,500
Carbon disulfite		8,000
Benzine		10,000
Miscellaneous		
Carbon to CO_2		14,093
Carbon to CO		4,347
Sulfur		3,983
Methane		23,879

From Combustion Engineering Inc.

26

Wood	-	8,420	Btu/lb
Brush	-	8,600	Btu/lb
Plastic	-	18,000	Btu/lb
Paper	-	7,900	Btu/lb
Garbage	-	7,280	Btu/lb

Although plastic could upset the situation as they grow in importance, the "family tree" of combustible materials in Figure 1-5 is based on a moisture and ash-free percentage of the material. Table 1-9 illustrates the relative quantities of air required and heat released from the various constituents in the combustion of refuse. To determine the necessary design parameters, the air and gas weight must be evaluated from an ultimate analysis. The ultimate analysis used in the sample calculations given below is as follows:

Carbon	-	30%
Oxygen	-	22%
Hydrogen	-	4%
Moisture	-	24%
Noncombustible	-	20%

It may be of interest to compare these selected compositions with the ranges found by various investigators:

Carbon   —   25% to 35%

Oxygen   —   15% to 30%

Hydrogen   —   3.5% to 4.5%

Moisture   —   15% to 20%

Ash, metals , and glass (noncombustible) - 15% to 25%.

Final design should be based on the highest average heating value expected; otherwise the design could result in an under-sized furnace volume or insufficient grate area.

Heat is usually expressed as million Btu/hr, which is the product of the fuel burned, in pound per hour times the heating value in Btu per lb (Btu/hr = lb/hr x Btu/lb).

In the following example the heating value is found to be approximately 5,000 Btu/lb as received, however, on a moisture and ash-free basis, the following results are obtained:

Carbon   —   53.5%

Oxygen   —   39.3

Hydrogen —   7.2%

With this information, upon examining Figure 1-5, we note that 53.5% carbon and 39.3% oxygen come out exactly on the refuse line for a combustible material, requiring 720 lbs of air per million Btu of proper combustion.

Table 1-9.
Combustion Equations

Combustible	Molecular Weight	Equation		Heat Release (Btu/lb) (High)	Theoretical Air (lb/lb of Fuel Element)
Carbon	12	$C + O_2$	$\rightarrow CO_2$	14,100	11.52
Hydrogen	2	$H_2 + 0.5\,O_2$	$\rightarrow H_2O$	61,100	34.50
Sulfur	32	$S + O_2$	$\rightarrow SO_2$	4,000	4.32
Hydrogen sulfide	34	$H_2S + 1.5\,O_2$	$\rightarrow SO_2 + H_2O$	7,100	3.10
Methane	16	$CH_4 + 2\,O_2$	$\rightarrow CO_2 + 2\,H_2O$	23,880	17.28
Ethane	30	$C_2H_6 + 3.5\,O_2$	$\rightarrow 2\,CO_2 + 3\,H_2O$	23,320	16.12
Propane	44	$C_3H_8 + 5\,O_2$	$\rightarrow 3\,CO_2 + 4\,H_2O$	21,660	15.63
Butane	58	$C_4H_{10} + 6.5\,O_2$	$\rightarrow 4\,CO_2 + 5\,H_2O$	21,300	15.48
Pentane	72	$C_5H_{12} + 8\,O_2$	$\rightarrow 5\,CO_2 + 6\,H_2O$	21,090	15.38

From Fernandes

29

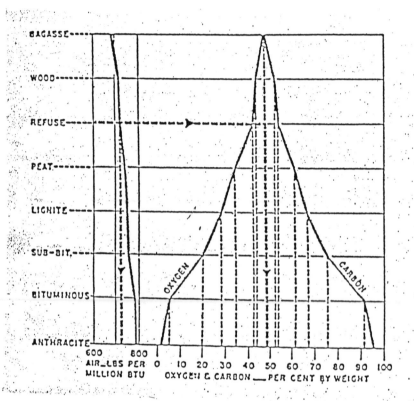

Figure]-5. Family Tree classification of combustible materials.
            Source: Fernandes.

Air and Gas Weight Determination

The refuse ultimate analysis chosen for the sample calculations requires the following theoretical air (see Table 1-9):

$$C \rightarrow 0.30 \ x11.54 \ = \ 3.46 \ lb \ air$$

$$(H \ -O/8) \rightarrow 4 \ -\left(\frac{22}{8}\right) x \ 34.56 \ = \ 0.43 \ lb \ air$$

$$Total \ = \ 3.89 \ lb \ dry \ air$$

Hence, the amount of theoretical atmospheric air to completely react with 1 lb of refuse is 3.89 lb. To insure complete combustion, 50% excess air is assumed. This can vary with the type of firing and whether the furnace is water cooled or not. Greater amounts may be used to dilute the products of combustion and control furnace temperature, but this air is not actually part of the combustion process. The total combustion air to be used with 50% excess air, regardless of how it is admitted to the burning zone (under- or overfeed air), is computed as 1.5 x 3.89 = 5.84 lb dry air per pound of refuse. This computation can be checked against Figure 1-6 if 5,000 Btu/lb refuse is converted to million Btu by dividing 5,000 into 1,000,000. It is then determined that there are 200 lbs of refuse, waste per million Btu. Introducing this to the preceding calculation (5.84 x 200), 1,168 lb of air per million Btu are to be used with 50% excess air. This compares with 1,070 lb. air per million Btu from Table 1-9,

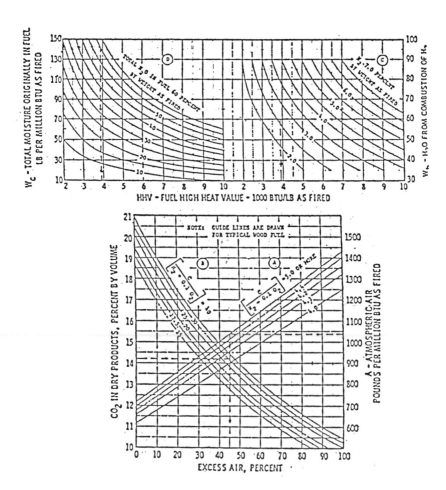

Figure]-6. C, H₂ and O₂ on combustible basis; plot are for wood and bagasse.
Source: Fernandes.

indicating a required air quantity of 8.4% below the computed estimate.

Another quick method of estimating the theoretical air for a refuse fuel is determined by estimating heating value (HHV) and substituting it into the formula

$$T \times A = 7.7 \times 10^{-4} \times HHV = \text{pounds of air per pound of refuse (6)}$$

The value obtained, 3.85 lb/lb, compares well with the computed value above. The constant in this equation (7.7×10^{-4}) varies somewhat with the variations in refuse composition. These results are good for rough design estimates.

The quantity of flue gas produced per unit mass of refuse in the above example can be determined from the foregoing results:

Carbon burned*	0.300
Hydrogen	0.040
Oxygen	0.220
Moisture	0.240
Dry combustion air (50% excess)	5.840
Weight of flue gas	6.640 lb gas per

lb. of refuse
(plus air
moisture)

* Note that for the carbon burned value, if combustion is incomplete, assume that the combustion exhibits a hydrogen preferen-

33

tial and the percent unburned combustible is entirely attribute to the carbon in the refuse. Once the unburned carbon is computed, correct the carbon burned to reflect this effect.

Products of Combustion

The 6.64 lb of flue gas per pound of refuse indicated is the total product minus air moisture when this is added to the total, wet products of combustion are obtained. The quantity of moisture in the flue gas can be computed as follows:

Assuming 0.020 lb moisture per pound of dry air used, 0.020 x 5.84 = 0.117 lb/lb of refuse. So, total products of combustion for this example are 6.64 + 0.12 = 6.76 lb/lb of refuse.

Moisture   0.24   = 0.24
Hydrogen, 0.04 x 9   = 0.36
Air moisture from above   = 0.12

                                              0.72

Total moisture in flue gas 0.72 lb/lb of refuse
The dry product of combustion can now be computed:
   6.76 - 0.72 = 6.04 lb/lb of refuse fired

The combustion of the gaseous products of the refuse can be computed as follows from the assumed ultimate analysis:

CO_2 = 0.30 x 3.67 = 1.10 lb/lb of refuse fired

H_2 (as computed above) = 0.72 lb/lb of refuse fired

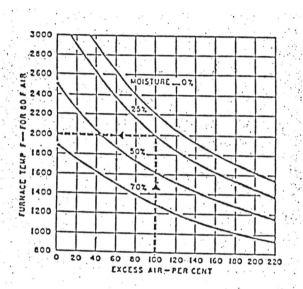

Figure 1-7. Plot of furnace gas temperature in a refractory
furnace as a function of excess air and moisture
level.
Source. Fernandes.

$$O_2 \left(3.89/2 \times 0.232\right) = 0.45 \text{ lb/lb of refuse fired}$$

$$N_2 (3.89 \times 0.769 \times 1.5) = 4.49 \text{ lb/lb of refuse fired}$$

This assumption depends on the inlet air conditions. In this case temperature = 80^0 F and relative humidity = 90%. The moisture value is then read from the psychrometric chart.

Total wet products of combustion of 1 lb of the assumed refuse equals 6.76 lb/lb of refuse. Therefore:

$$CO_2 = \frac{1.10}{6.76} = 0.163 \text{ lb/lb of flue gas}$$

$$H_2O = \frac{0.72}{6.76} = 0.106 \text{ lb/lb of flue gas}$$

$$O_2 = \frac{0.45}{6.76} = 0.067 \text{ lb/lb of flue gas}$$

$$N_2 = \frac{4.49}{6.76} = 0.664 \text{ lb/lb of flue gas}$$

Total = 1.000 lb/lb of flue gas

This can be expressed on a dry basis:

1.000 − 0.106 = 0.894 lb/lb of refuse (dry)

$$CO_2 = \frac{0.163}{0.894} = 0.182 \text{ lb/lb of dry flue gas}$$

$$O_2 = \frac{0.067}{0.894} = 0.075 \text{ lb/lb of dry flue gas}$$

$$N_2 = \frac{0.664}{0.894} = 0.743 \text{ lb/lb of dry flue gas}$$

Total = 1.000

Volumetric composition of the dry products of combustion:

$$CO_2 = \frac{0.182}{44} = 0.00413 \qquad \frac{4.13}{32.87} = 0.126 = 12.6\%$$

$$O_2 = \frac{0.075}{32} = 0.00234 \qquad \frac{2.34}{32.87} = 0.071 = 7.1\%$$

$$N_2 = \frac{0.743}{28} = 0.02640 \qquad \frac{26.4}{32.87} = 0.803 = 80.3\%$$

Moles of dry gas = 0.03287   100%

36

If the CO_2 concentration is less than just indicated, the oxygen will be greater, indicating greater than 50% excess air should be used in the system. Conversely, a greater volume of CO_2 and less oxygen means that less than 50% excess air should be used.

Furnace temperature, an important parameter in the design of incinerators, is the temperature of the flue gases leaving t h e furnace. This can be approximated by determining an average specific heat and using it to compute the temperature.

The furnace exit temperature can be estimated from Figure 1-7. Using 24% moisture and 50% excess air used in the example, the temperature is found to be approximately $2,500^\circ$ F.

The specific heat of CO_2 at constant pressure varies from 8.89 to 14.16 Btu/1m-mole$^\circ$F between 80° F to $2,500^\circ$ F. For an average of 11.53 Btu/lb-mole$^\circ$ F or 0.262 Btu/lb - $^\circ$ F.

Similarly for

Moisture   0.545   Btu/lb - $^\circ$F

Oxygen   0.247

Nitrogen   0.274

The temperature is computed as follows:

$$[(WC_p) + (WC_p) + (WC_p) + (WC_p)] (T_2 - T)$$
$$\quad CO_2 \quad\quad H_2O \quad\quad O_2 \quad\quad N_2$$

i.e., $\Sigma WC_p(T_2 - T)$

$$CO_2 = 0.163 \times 0.262 = 0.0427$$
$$H_2O = 0.106 \times 0.545 = 0.0577$$
$$O_2 = 0.067 \times 0.247 = 0.0166$$
$$N_2 = 0.664 \times 0.274 = 0.1820$$
$$\Sigma WC_p = 0.2990$$

37

The furnace inlet temperature assumed here is 80° F.

The heat released and made available to the furnace per pound of refuse will be assumed as 4.70 Btu/lb. This assumes a 5% heat loss in incomplete combustion and through the furnace wall. Dividing by 6.76 lb of flue gas/lb of refuse, gives 703 Btu/lb of flue gas. The estimated furnace exit temperature is:

$$(T_{exit} - 540) = \frac{703}{0.299} = 2350 \tag{7}$$

$$T_{exit} = 2350 + 540$$
$$= 2890^\circ \text{ R}$$
$$= 2430^\circ \text{ F}$$

Combustion

Fossil fuels along with waste fuels contain three significant combustible elements -- carbon, hydrogen, and sulfur. Sulfur oxidation is only a minor source of heat but may be a significant air pollution problem due to sulfur dioxide formation. During **complete** combustion, the hydrogen and carbon constituents of the fuel combine with the oxygen in air as follows:

$$2 \; H_2 + O_2 \rightarrow H_2O + 61,100 \text{ Btu/lb. of } H_2 \text{ combusted}$$
$$C + O_2 \rightarrow CO_2 + 14,100 \text{ Btu/lb of C combusted}$$

The term "complete" combustion assumes the above reactions go to to completion. However, not all of the Btu's in a fuel are

38

connected to heat. Some fuel may go unburned resulting in carbon in the ash or hydrocarbons exiting the stack as air emissions. Carbon may be incompletely combusted forming Carbon Monoxide (CO) instead of CO_2. To assume sufficient oxygen is present to combine with the carbon and hydrogen in the fuel it is necessary to provide more than the stoichemetric oxygen requirement. Excess air is therefore introduced into the combustion process because it is impossible to get a perfect union of oxygen and fuel. The quantity of excess air is kept at a minimum in order to hold down the loss of heat from the stack.

In order for complete combustion of hydrogen fuels to occur, there are several factors that must be examined and are generally termed the three T's of combustion -- temperature, time, and turbulence as was discussed in Chapter 1. The importance of these basic conditions is worthy of repetition.

Temperature -- Two temperaturres are a concern in assuring complete combustion. First "ignition temperature" is defined as the temperature at which more heat is generated by combustion then is lost to the surroundings. In effect, it is the temperature in which fuel combustion becomes self-sustaining. The ignition temperatures of waste fuels vary greatly and factors such as pressure, velocity, air to fuel mixture uniformity, firebox configuration, and the presence of catalysts may influence the ignition temperature of individual fuel components. Secondly, "adiabatic flame temperature" is defined as the theoretical maximum temperature produced by complete combustion of the fuel with no heat loss. Obviously the heat combustion of the fuel is the leading factor in determining the flame temperature. However, increasing the temperature of the fuel or combustion air also increases the flame temperature in the firebox.

Time - The time factor in combustion refers to the length of time the fuel / air mixture is exposed to an adequate temperature promoting combustion. Combustion engineers refer to this time as the "residence time". Combustion is not an instantaneous process. If the rate of combustion is slower than the rate of heat loss (to the surroundings), incomplete combustion may result due to cooling of the combustion gases. When examining hydrocarbon destruction efficiency of a boiler combusting waste fuels, a residence time calcualation must be performed. Factors that affect residence time include firebox area, temperature profile of the firebox, and volumetric flow through the firebox.

Turbulence - The turbulence factor in the combustion process refers to the mixing of the air and fuel in the combustion chamber. Without complete mixing, complete combustion cannot occur. Adequate turbulence is achieved by both fuel nozzle selection and by firebox chamber design.

Solid Waste as a Potential Fuel

Wastes in most cases are heterogenous. Thus the characteristics must be carefully defined before an application as an energy source can be chosen. The following should be determined for any waste to be burned, expecially in consideration for use as a fuel:

1. Moisture content
2. Volatile matter content
3. Fixed carbon content
4. Ash content
5. Heating value
6. Corrosiveness
7. Toxicity
8. Odor
9. Explosiveness
10. Flash point
11. Density
12. Ash-fusion temperature
13. Viscosity
14. Ultimate Analysis

    C

    H

    N

    Metals, Etc.

Processing wastes can become very complex as we search for the most economical, yet efficient system. A waste disposal, volume reduction, and combustion system must consider many factors including:

1. Segregation
2. Transportation
3. Solid and liquid preparation
4. Storage and equalization
5. Handling and feeding
6. Combustion process requirement
7. Corrosiveness or other facility damage
8. Residue handling and disposal
9. Environmental impact.
10. Regulatory compliance.

TABLE I-10.
LISTING OF COMMON WASTES WITH FUEL VALUE (AVERAGE)

	BTU/LB, AS FIRED
GAS	
Coke-oven gas	19,700
Blast-furnace gas	1,139
CO gas	575
Refinery gas	21,800
LIQUID	
Industrial sludge	3700-4200
Black liquor	4,400
Sulfite liquor	4,200
Dirty solvents	10,000-16,000
Spent lubricants	10,000-14,000
Paints and resins	6,000-10,000
Oil waste, fuel oil residue	18,000
SOLID	
Bagasse	3,600-6,500
Bark	4,500-5,200
General wood wastes	4,500-6,500
Sawdust and shavings	4,500-7,500
Coffee grounds	4,900-6,500
Nut hulls	7,700
Rice hulls	5,225-6,500
Corn cobs	8,000-8,300
Boot, shoe trim and scrap	8,500
Sponge waffle and scrap	8,500
Butyl soles scrap	11,500
Cement wet scrap	11,500
Rubber	12,420
Tire cord scrap	12,400
Tires, bus and auto	18,000
Gum scrap	19,700
Latex waste, coagulum waste	12,000
Leather scrap	10,000
Waxed paper	12,000
Cork scrap	12,400
PLASTIC AND SYNTHETIC REFUSE	
Cellophane plastic	12,000
Polyethylene	19,840
Polyvinyl chloride	17,500
Vinyl scrap	17,500
Aldehyde sludge	18,150
Solvent naptha	18,500
Carbon disulfite	8,000
Benzine	10,000

43

REFERENCES

American Public Works Association, Public Administration Service, **Refuse Collection Practice,** 3rd ed., Washington, DC (1966).

Bailie, R.C., Donner, D.M., and Galli, A.F., Proc. 1968 **Nat. Incinerator Conference,** New York, 12-17 (1968).

Cheremisinoff, N.P., and Azbel, D.S., **Fluid Mechanics and Unit Operations,** Ann Arbor Science Pub., Ann Arbor, MI 1983.

Cheremisinoff, N.P., and Cheremisinoff, P.N., **Hydrodynamics of Gas-Solid Flows,** Gulf Pub. Co., Houston, TX, 1984.

Cheremisinoff, P.N., and Young, R.A., **Pollution Engineering Practice Handbook,** Ann Arbor Science Pub., Ann Arbor, MI, 1975.

Cross, F., **Handbook of Incineration,** Technomic Publishing Co., Lancaster, PA (1972)

Fernandes, J.H. **"Incinerator Air Pollution Control,"**, Paper presented at the National Incinerator Conference, ASME, NY, (1968).

Orning, A.A., **Principles of Combustion,** Wiley-Interscience Pub. Co., NY, 1969.

"Technical – Economic Study of Solid Waste Disposal Needs and Practices," Combustion Engineering Inc., for U.S. PHS. – PH86-66-133.

PARTICULATE CAPTURE

Incineration operations produce a variety of emissions in the form of particulate matter and odorous and noxious gases. It is common practice therefore, to employ collection devices to decrease such emissions and to ensure maximum combustion efficiency. Because of the variable nature of the materials charged to incinerators and the changing modes of operation, the rate of particulate emissions can vary widely. For example, in the incineration of municipal wastes, typical emission values range from at 3 to 5 lb per ton to 10 to 25 lb per ton of refuse burned. There is general agreement, however, that the size of particulates is quite small. Particles emitted from incinerators range from less than 5 micron (0.0002 in.) to about 120 microns (0.005 in.) in diameter. These fall into the category of fine dusts, as shown by the particle classification in Figure 2-1.

The removal of particles smaller than 50 microns is difficult and requires efficient collecting devices. Conventional **particle capturing devices** are based on gravity settling, inertia or momentum, filtration or electrostatic precipitation and agglomeration via sonic mechanical means to facilitate removal by increasing particle size. Both wet and dry media can be employed in most of these devices. To control or eliminate objectionable

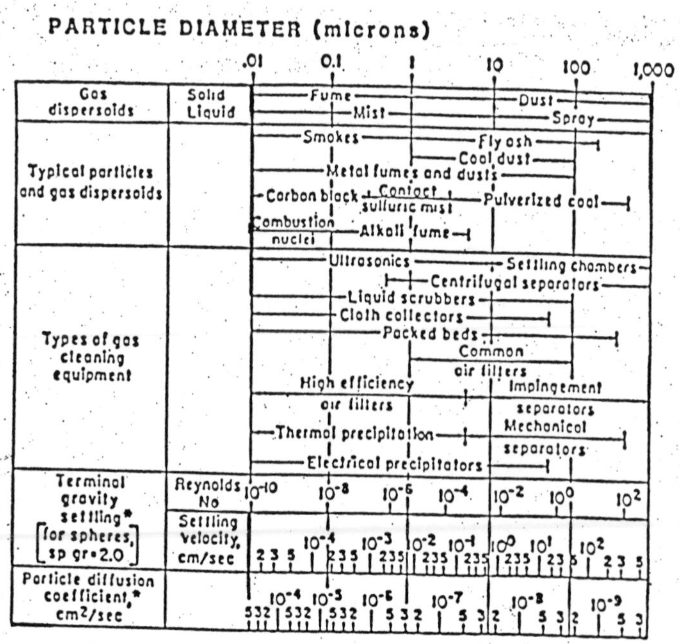

Figure 2-1. Particle size classification chart.

odors in circumstances where they cannot otherwise be readily handled, secondary combustion with or without catalysts, and wet scrubbing are employed.

Particles entrained in gas streams are subject to several forces and actions (e.g., settling is induced due to the influence of gravity, particles collide with each other and agglomerate, impinge on obstacles such as walls, baffles, and liquid droplets, or attract small entities). By utilizing those forces and enhancing them with centrifugal, electrostatic, and sonic actions, separation of the particles from gas streams is achieved.

Particle dynamics is a complex subject, primarily due to the inability to adequately describe particle-particle interactions. We can, however, gain some insight on the dominant forces that must be accounted for in design by reviewing the behavior of single particles. Consider the limiting case of free fall of a single spherical particle. When there is relative motion between a fluid and a particle immersed in that fluid, such as with free-falling solids, drag forces are exerted on the particle. These forces are caused by skin friction and the differential pressure upstream and downstream of the particle resulting from the change in the stream lines of the gas flowing past the obstacle.

A free-falling particle accelerates until the frictional drag of the fluid surrounding the particle balances the gravitational force. From this point the particle continues to fall at a constant velocity, or at its terminal velocity. The terminal velocity of a free-falling sphere is expressed by the following free balance:

$$f = \frac{\pi}{g} C_D \rho_f d_p^2 U_t^2 V_p (\rho_p - \rho_f) g \tag{1}$$

From when the terminal velocity is:

$$U_t^2 = \frac{8 V_p (\rho_p - \rho_f) g}{C_D \rho_f d_p^2 \pi} \tag{2}$$

where f = drag force
       C_D = drag coefficient
       ρ = fluid density
       d_p = particle diameter
       U_t = terminal velocity of particle
       V_p = particle volume
       ρ_p = particle density
       g = gravitational constant

Since the volume of a sphere is $V_p = (\pi d_p^3 / 6)$,   then

$$U_t^2 = \frac{4}{3} \frac{d_p (\rho_p - \rho_f) g}{\rho_f C_D} \tag{3}$$

The drag coefficient C_D is a function of the Reynolds number, which in turn is related to the diameter of the particle. The three ranges of Reynolds numbers considered in determining the drag coefficient are summarized in Table 2-1.

48

For settling in the laminar regime, frictional drag dominates, and from Table 2-1

$$C_D = 24/Re = \frac{24\,\mu_f}{d_p U \rho_f} \qquad (4)$$

Substituting for C_D in Equation 3 gives the terminal settling velocity for laminar conditions:

$$U_t = \frac{g d_p^2 (\rho_p - \rho_f)}{18\,\mu_f} \qquad (5)$$

where

d_p = particle diameter
U_t = terminal velocity of particle
V_p = particle volume
ρ_p = particle density
g = gravitational constant

Equation 4 is the Stokes law expression for the terminal settling velocity of a particle. The preceding relationship is based on a single sphere falling in a limitless gas expense unhindered by other particles or boundary surfaces.

A plot of drag coefficient versus Reynolds number for spheres, disks, and cylinders is shown in Figure 2-2. Very small particles, whose diameters approach the mean free path of the gas

49

TABLE 2-1
Drag Coefficients for a Sphere

Reynolds Number Range	$10^{-4} \sim 10$ (Stokes Law)	$10 \sim 1,000$ (Transition)	$1,000 \sim 10^5$ (Newton Law)
Drag coefficient, C_D	$24/Re$	$f(Re)$	0.43
Setling Velcocity, u_t	$\dfrac{g\Delta\rho d p^2}{18\mu_f}$	$\left(\dfrac{4\Delta\rho d_p g}{3C_D \rho_f}\right)^{1/2}$	$1.7\left(\dfrac{\Delta\rho d_p g}{\rho_f}\right)^{1/2}$
Controlling resistance	Frictional	Friction plus Shape	Shape

From Cheremlslnoff and Cheremlslnoff

TABLE 2-2.
Cunningham Correction Factors

Particle Diameter (microns)	Cunningham Correction
0.01	22.35
0.1	2.87
1.00	1.16
10.00	1.016
20.00	1.008

Mean free path of the fluid molecules, λ, is 6.53×10^{-6} cm.
From Zenz and Othmer

TABLE 2-3
Displacement Ratio for Various Sizes of Particles In Air

Particle Size (Microns)	Displacement Ratio
0.1	17
0.5	0.45
1.00	0.09
5.00	0.002

From McCormlc, Lucas, and Wells

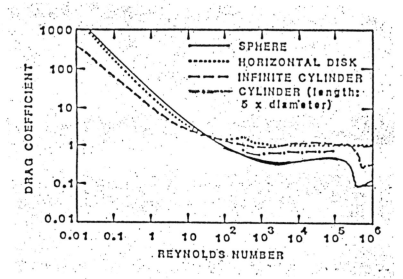

Figure 2-2. Plot drag coefficients vs. Reynolds number.

molecules, fall faster than predicted by Stokes law. This occurs because the particles slip between the gas molecules. The Cunningham correction factor is applied to Stokes law for such particles and results in the following expression for calculating terminal velocity (V_t):

$$U_t = \frac{g d_p^2 (\rho_p - \rho_f)}{18\,\mu_f}\left(1 + \frac{k\lambda}{d_p}\right) \tag{6}$$

where K is a constant ranging from 1.25 to 2.3 for different gases and particles sizes and   is the mean free path of the fluid molecules. As shown in Table 2-2 corrections for small particles in air are significant, however, this correction approaches unity with increasing size.

Effect of Brownian Motion

Another factor that affects the settling of small particles is random Brownian motion resulting from particle bombardment by the gas molecules. The Brownian effect is significant for particles of 1 micron in size and smaller, and becomes increasingly important as the size of the particle decreases. A measure of the effect of Brownian motion is the displacement ratio, which is defined as the ratio of the random movement of a falling particle due to variation of the displacement ratio with size for particles falling in the air is shown in Table 2-3. A general formula

52

expressing the displacement of the particles due to Brownian forces based on the theoretical derivation by Einsten is:

$$x = \left[\left(\frac{2RT}{N}\right)\left(\frac{t}{3\pi\mu_f d_p}\right)\left(1+\frac{K\lambda}{d_p}\right)\right]^{1/2} \tag{7}$$

where   R = the gas constant
       T = the absolute temperature
       N = Avogadro's number

       t = time
      μ_f = gas viscosity
      d_p = particle diameter
  $(1+K\lambda/d_p)$ = the Cunningham correction factor

For settling in air at 20° C the equation is $\qquad\qquad$ (8)

$$x = 6.8\left[\frac{t}{d_p}\left(1+\frac{K\lambda}{d_p}\right)\right]^{1/2}$$

where x = average displacement (microns)
    d_p = particle diameter (microns)
    t = time (sec)

Particle Agglomeration

Agglomeration of micron and submicron particles into a cluster as a result of collision and adherence often can facilitate removal from a gas stream. The factors that effect agglomeration of small particles are particle size, the nature surface of the particles surfaces, the presence of absorbed gases on their surfaces, the rate of dispersion, humidity, and possibly the temperature and viscosity of the gas medium. As an approach to understanding the adhesion of particles, Bradley and Hamaker derived an expression for the adhesive force between two bodies based on London-van der Waals forces of attraction as follows:

$$f = \frac{(\pi^2 q_0^2 \lambda')(d_1 d_2)}{12x^2(d_1 + d_2)} \tag{9}$$

where f = force of attraction (dynes)
q_0 = number of atoms per cubic centimeter of the substance
λ' = van der Waals constant

Brownian coagulation of smokes was studied intensively by Whytlaw et al. where the following empirical expression was derived:

$$\frac{1}{n} - \frac{1}{n_o} = K_B t \tag{10}$$

where n = number of particles per c.c. at time t

54

n_o = the original concentration

K_B = the agglomeration constant

Particle Adhesion

Adhesion of small particles to solid surfaces is another aspect of particle dynamics and is important in separation techniques such as filtration, impaction, and electrostatic precipitation. Factors that influence adhesion are particle size and shape, particle and surface material, surface roughness, temperature, and humidity of the ambient gas, time of particle-surface contact, and electrostatic forces. Corn investigated the effects of several of these variables on the force of adhesion of Quartz and Pyrex-glass particles with diameters ranging from 20 to 90 microns on a flat Pyrex slide and on a glass microscope slide. His findings are summarized as:

- Effect of particle size - The force of adhesion is proportional to particle size.
- Effect of relative humidity - Adhesion increases with increasing relative humidity.
- Effect of surface roughness - Adhesion decreases with increased surface roughness.

Corn's expreiments for adhesion of quartz particles to pyrex plates were correlated by the expression

$$S = 8.8 \times 10^3 e^{-0.053A} \qquad (11)$$

where   S = average surface roughness in Angstroms

         A = percent of adhesion

- Effect of particle-surface contact time - The force of adhesion was not significantly altered by the time of contact if the contact time was at least 5 minutes.

Impingement

Removal of dust particles by impingement is utilized principally in filtration devices, baffled chambers, and wet scrubbers. Separation of particles occurs because their inertia contained in a flowing gas exceeds that of the gas. Consider the example in Figure 2-3, where a gas moving at a velocity U flows past a cylinder of diameter D. Particles contained in the portion of gas stream will impinge onto the exposed target's surface area. The particle's inertia is defined as the change in motion and is equal to the product of the force which is attempting to create a change in the direction of motion and the time through which it is attempting to create a change in the direction of motion and the time through which it acts. The generalized target efficiency equation for any single-stage impaction capture is:

$$\eta = \exp- \left\{ \frac{0.018}{D} \psi'^{0.5+R} - 0.6\,R'^2 \right\} \qquad (12a)$$

56

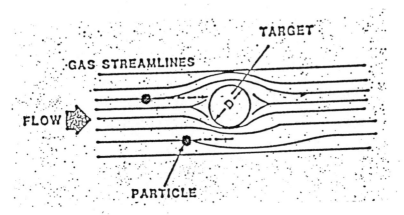

Figure 2-3.   Illustrates impingement of particles onto a target.

where η = effective target efficiency

D = collector surface diameter

R' = ratio of particle diameter to collector diameter

ψ' = dimensionless impaction parameter, defined as

$$\psi' = \left\{ \frac{C\rho_p v_r d_p^2}{18\mu D} \right\}^{1/2} \tag{12b}$$

where v_r is the relative velocity of the particles with respect to the target and C is a slip velocity correction factor for particles less than 1 um in size:

$$C = 1 + \frac{3.45 \times 10^{-4} T}{d_p} \tag{13}$$

where T = absolute temperature ($^{\circ}$R) and d_p is particle size in microns. Equation 13 is applicable over the Reynolds number range between 0.04 to 1.4.

Wet Scrubbers

A wide range of wet scrubbers is available for control of particulates as well as gases from effluent gas streams. Table 2-4 shows a summary of basic types of scrubbers for particulate control.

Air Emissions

Emission Characteristics - The combustion of specific

58

wastes oils and solvents in industrial boilers must be closely examined from an air emissions standpoint. Until recently, very little documentation regarding the extent to which chemical contaminants or hydrocarbon constituents in waste fuels are destroyed or altered during combustion was available.

In 1984, the United States Environmental Protection Agency (USEPA) conducted a comprehensive study of the air emission impacts from the disposal of waste oils by combustion in commercial boilers (Fennelly). In this study, actual stack tests were conducted on boilers in the size range of 0.4 to 25 million Btu/hr. Seven boilers were selected for testing in the program. The units were chosen so as to provide a representative cross section of the types and sizes of various boilers. A 4,000 - gallon supply of used automotive oil was obtained and served as a consistent supply of waste fuel for the program. Some of the stock oil was spiked with measured amounts of selected organic compounds which are typically found in waste fuels. The selected organic compounds were chloroform, 1,1,1-trichloroethane, trichloroethylene, tetrachloroethylene, trichlorobenzene, 1-chloronapthathalene, 2,4,5-trichlorophenol, and chlorotoluene. Stack testing was conducted at each of the sites to determine the atmospheric emissions of particulates (principally lead) inorganic compounds (principally HCl), and volatile organic compounds. The destruction efficiencies for each of the spiked components

59

TABLE 2-4. SUMMARY OF BASIC TYPES OF SCRUBBERS

BASIC TYPE	SPECIFIC TYPE	WATER VS. GAS FLOW	WATER CIRCU-LATION gpm per 1000 cfm	DRAFT LOSS Inches water gauge	PERCENT COLLECTION EFFICIENCY ON FINE DUST		
					Low	Moderate	High
	tangential inlet wet cyclone	concurrent or cross	3 - 5	1 - 4	X	X	
Impingement Baffle	spiral baffle wet cyclone	concurrent	1 - 2	4 - 6	X	X	
	single plate	concurrent	2 - 4	1 - 8	X	X	
	multiple plate	concurrent	3 - 5	6 - 12	X	X	
	fixed bed	concurrent or counter	10 - 20	2 - 4	X		
Packed Tower	fluidized bed	counter	15 - 30	4 - 12	X	X	
	flooded bed	concurrent	2 - 4	4 - 8		X	
	multiple bed	counter	20 - 40	4 - 12			

(TABLE 2-4 CONTINUED)

Submerged Orifice	wide slot		15 – 30	2 – 15	X	X	
	circular slot	concurrent	15 – 30	2 – 15	X	X	
	multiple slot		15 – 30	2 – 15	X	X	
	high-pressure		5 – 7	30 – 100			X
Venturi	medium-pressure	cross or	3 – 5	10 – 30		X	X
	low-pressure	concurrent	2 – 4	3 – 10	X	X	
	flooded disc		5 – 6	30 – 70		X	X
	cross-flow packed	cross	1 – 4	2 – 4	X	X	
Miscellaneous and Combination Scrubbers	centrifugal fan		1 – 2	(a)	X	X	
	multiple venturi		4 – 6	20 – 80		X	X
	combination venturi	concurrent	5 – 7	15 – 60		X	X
	combination fan type		2 – 3	(a)		X	

61

were also determined.

From the results of this study, it is possible to make some general conclusions concerning the combustion of waste automotive crankcase oil in boilers of this size range.

Emissions of lead and other metals including arsenic, cadmium, and chromium, are significant and of immediate concern. Most of the lead emissions are submicron in size and there readily inhalable. Material balance calculations indicate that 50 to 60 percent of the lead introduced into a boiler exits from the system via the stack. Analysis of the ash collected in the firebox indicates lead levels of up to 2 percent. This provided an accounting mass balance of only 65 percent of the lead consumed. National Ambient Air Quality Standards (NAAQS) for lead may possibly be violated in the impact areas surrounding an industrial boiler combusting pure automotive waste oils (castaldini).

It is possible to achieve **hydrocarbon combustion** efficiencies greater than 99.9 percent for industrial boilers firing waste oils. For the spiked halogenated organic compounds typically found in trace quantities in waste oils, destruction efficiencies greater than 99.9 percent are obtainable.

Particulate emission from the six boilers tested ranged from 0.97 to 1.2 lbs/hr (0.34 lb/million Btu heat input). This is significantly higher than the EPA's own emission factors of 0.09 lb/million Btu for commercial boilers firing residual oils (EPA 1977). However, the higher value is consistent with the much higher ash content of waste oil, which can range from 0.15 percent to 1.5 percent (Cotton).

In the **boilers** tested that were above one million Btu/hr capacity, there was no apparent correlation between boiler size or firing method and hydrocarbon destruction efficiency.

Polychlorinated dioxin (PCDD) and **chlorinated dibenzofuran (PCDF)** species were detected in 60 percent of the boiler stack samples. The concentrations of these toxic particulate contaminants ranged from 7 to 470 parts per trillion (ppt). Tests were also completed on samples of the waste fuel to determine PCDD and PCDF levels prior to combustion. No dioxin or dibenzofuran compounds were detected in any of the oil samples. Therefore, dioxin and dibenzofuran found in the boiler stack samplind were probably formed during the combustion process. The fly ash deposited inside the boilers may contain parts per billion levels of chlorinated dibenzofuran and dioxin compounds. The ash has the potential for being classified as hazardous on this basis, and may be subject to stringent RCRA regulations for disposal. The whole dioxin issue is not specific to industrial boilers burning waste fuels. Dioxins are an important environmental issue in assessing the impacts of garbage burning resource recovery plants, and hazardous waste incinerators. It has been said that tetrachlorodibenzodioxin (TCDD) is the most hazardous chemical ever made by mankind. The extent to which the family of PCDD and PCDF compounds pose a hazard at the low levels found in the stack gas of industrial boilers burning waste fuels is undetermined. Risk assessment experts, industrial hygienists, and air pollution modeling experts will key in on this issue in the very near future.

Halogen based acid gas emissions from the boilers tested were significant. Halogen elements include chlorine, bromine, and flourine. These elements when present in waste fuels usually form hydrogen chloride, hydrogen bromide, or hydrogen flouride in the flue gas when combusted. These compounds are all acid gases that present both localized and long-range transport air pollution problems (Olexsey).

Control of "acid rain" is a key issue on both the State and Federal regulatory levels. As previously mentioned, combustion of waste fuels with high halogen levels without acid gas scrubbers is illegal.

Instrumentation - The quantity of oxygen in the flue gas is a good indicator of the status of an incinerator or boiler's combustion process. The presence of oxygen indicates that excess air is being introduced. In operation, it is necessary to provide a system to allow automatic proportioning of the quantity of air to the quantity of fuel. The three types of combustion controllers used include: fuel - flow air - flow, and gas - flow analysis. The type of incinerator boiler and the fuel properties must be examined to determine the best guide for a particular unit. A combination is sometimes incorporated in the instrumentation system.

Air Emission Control Devices - Industrial boilers that fire either conventional or waste fuels are generally not equipped with any air pollution control devices (APCD's). However, with todays rising cost of hazardous waste disposal of many spent solvents, it is becoming increasingly attractive (cost effective) to consider adding an APCD to allow boiler combustion of a waste fuel stream that may not meet the USEPA and NJDEP requirements for **uncontrolled** boiler combustion. Particulate control devices have been discussed previously.

Two criteria pollutants that may present a need for control are: particulates, and hydrogen chloride (HCl). As previously discussed, particulate emissions stem from the ash content of the fuel and HCl emissions from a waste's halogen content. Let us examine three potential scenarios where installation of APCD's would be required:

1) The waste stream does not contain significant ash (<.2%) by weight. However, the halogen content of the fuel exceeds 0.1% by weight. In this example, a packed column absorber (scrubber)

65

will be required for HCl removal. An important point ot note is that excessive HCl generated during the combustion process may cause **extreme** boiler tube or incinerator wall corrosion if the flue gas in is allowed to drop below the dew point of HCl. This is an important design and operating parameter to examine when considering combustion of a waste fuel high in organically bound chlorine, bromine, or flourine.

2) The waste stream contains no organically bound chlorine or halogens. However, the waste fuel contains ash in excess of 0.2% by weight. If the State and Federal regulations require a particulate removal efficiency between 95 to 99%, an electrostatic precipitator (ESP) becomes a likely choice of a particulate emission control device. If a removal efficiency in excess of 99.5% is required, a baghouse is a more cost effective choice for particulate control.

3) The waste stream contains both significant ash (<0.2%) and significant halogen content (> 0.1%). In this example, a venturi scrubber/packed column absorption system would most likely be selected as the APCD's.

REFERENCES

Bradley, R.S., **"The Cohesive Forces Between Solid Surfaces and the Surface Energy of Solids,"** Phil. Mag., 13: 853-862.

Castaldini, C.; Unnasch, S.; Mason, H.B. Engineering Assessment Report -- Hazardous Waste Co-Firing in Industrial Boilers, Volume 2, Data Supplement, Sponsor: EPA, Cincinnati, OH. Hazardous Waste Engineering Research Lab., Report No. EPA/600/2-84/177B, Nov. 84.

Cheremisinoff, N.P., and Azbel, D.S., **Fluid Mechanics and Unit Operations,** Ann Arbor Science Pub., Ann Arbor, MI, 1983.

Cheremisinoff, P.N., and Young, R.A., **Pollution Engineering Practice Handbook,** Ann Arbor Science Pub., Ann Arbor, MI, 1975.

Corn, M., **"The Adhesion of Solid Particles to Solid Surfaces II,"** J.A.P.C.A., 11 (12): 566-584 (Dec. 1961).

Cotton, F. O.; Whisman, M. L.; Goetzinger, J.W.; Reynolds, J. W. **"Analysis of 30 Used Motor Oils,** Hydrocarbon Processing, 56(9):131-140, Sept. 1977.

Einstein, A., **"Elemental Theory of Brownian Motion,"** 41-42 (1907).

Fennelly, P.F.: McCabe, M.: Hall, J.M.; Kozik, M.F.; Hoyt, M.P., **"Envoronmental Characterization of Disposal of Waste Oils by Combustion in Small Commercial Boilers",** Report (GCA/TR/83-72-G, EPA/600/2-84/150), 1984.

Flood, L.P., J.A.P.C.A., 9 (1): 63-68 (May 1959).

Hamaker, H.C., **"The London-van der Walls Attraction Between Spherical Particles",** Physica, 4: 1058-1072 (1937).

Hitchcock, D., **"Solid -Waste Disposal -Incineration,"** Chemical Engineering (May 21, 1979).

"Hydrosystems for Liquid and Fume Incineration," BSP Div., Envirotech Corp., Belmont, CA, Bull. ESI 300-3-73-SM (1980).

Lapple, C.E., **"Fine Particle Characteristics,"** Standford Research Institute Journal, 5:95, (Third Quarter 1961).

Loeb, L.B., **"Kinetic Theory of Gases,"** McGraw-Hill Book Co., NY, 1934.

McCormic, P.Y., Lucas, R.L., and Wells, D.F., **"Gas-Solid Systems,"** Section 20, in Chekical Engineer's Handbook, 4th ed., R.H. Perry, C.H. Chilton and S.D. Kirkpatrick (Eds.), McGraw-Hill Book Co., NY, 1934.

Olexsey, R.A. **"Air Emissions from Industrial Boilers Burning Hazardous Waste Materials,"** Report (EPA/600/D-84/233; Order No. PB85-102879/GAR), 19 pp., 1984.

Stevens, J.L., Crumpler, E.P., and Shih, C.C., **"Thermal Destruction of Chemical Wastes,"** 71st Annual AIChE meeting (Nov. 14, 1978).

USEPA **"Compilation of Air Pollution Emission Factors,"** Third Edition Publication No. AP-42, US Govt. Printing Office, Washington, D.C. Stock No. 055-003-00087-4, Aug. 1977.

Warner, A., Parker, C.H., and Baum, B., **"Solid Waste Management of Plastics,"** Report of a Research Study for the Manufacturing Chemists Assoc., NY, 1970.

Whytlaw-Gray, R., and Patterson, H.S., Smoke, Edward Arnold Co., london, 1962.

Zenz, F.A., and Othmer, D.F., **"Fluidization and Fluid Particle Systems,"** Reinhold Publishing Co., NY, 1960.

3.

INCINERATOR TYPES

Incinerator Configurations

Empirical design methodology that has evolved from incinerator investigations has resulted in the development of two basic types of multiple-chamber incinerators, namely, the retort type and the in-line type. Other incinerator configurations include incinerators with vertically arranged chambers, L-shaped u;its, and units with separated chambers breeched together. These configurations are basically variations of the two basic designs. Each configuration has certain characteristics with respect to construction and operation, as well as limits to its applications. Figure 3-1 shows a cutaway view of typical retort multiple-chamber incinerator. This type of unit derives its name from the return flow of effluent through the U - shaped gas path and the side-by-side arrangement of component chambers. Figure 3-2 shows a typical in-line design, so called because the various chambers follow one another in a line. In both types of multiple-chamber incinerators the combustion process proceeds in two stages, that is primary or solid-phase, combustion in the ignition chamber, followed by secondary or gaseous-phase, combustion. The secondary combustion zone is composed of two parts: down draft or mixing chamber, and an up-pass expansion, or final

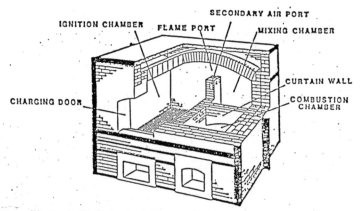

Figure 3-1 Retort-type multiple-chamber incinerator.

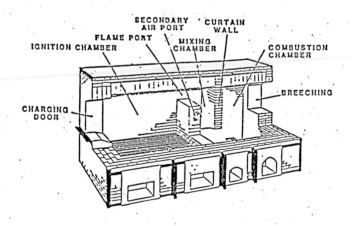

Figure. 3-2 Shows in-line multiple-chamber incinerator.

combustion chamber. The gas flow and the combustion reactions in the two-stage process proceeds as follows.

The ignition-chamber reaction includes the drying, ignition and combustion of the solid refuse. As the burning proceeds the moisture and volatile component of the fuel are vaporized and partially oxidized in passing from the ignition chamber into the mixing chamber.

From the flame port the products of combustion and the volatile components of the refuse flow through the mixing chamber, at which point secondary air is introduced. The combination of elevated temperatures and the addition of combustion air, augmented by the mixing chamber, or secondary burners as necessary, assist in promoting the second stage of combustion process. Turbulent mixing, resulting from restricted flow areas and abrupt changes in flow direction, furthers the gaseous-phase reaction. In passing through the curtain-wall port from the mixing chamber to the final combustion chamber the gases undergo additional changes in direction, accompanied by expansion and final oxidation of combustible components. Fly ash and other solid particulate matter are collected in the combustion chamber by wall impingement and simple setting. The gases finally discharge through a stack or, in some installations, through a combination of a gas cooler (e.g., a water-spray chamber or scrubber) and induced draft system.

Other incinerator configurations in use for thermally decomposing chemical process industry wastes are:

- Multiple-hearth furnaces.

- Fluidized-bed incinerators.

- Liquid-waste incinerators.

- Waste-gas flares.

- Direct-flame incinerators.

- Catalytic combusters.

- Rotary kilns.

- Wet-air oxidation units.

- Molten-salt incinerators.

- Multiple-chamber incinerators

- Ship-mounted incinerators.

Each of these devices has advantages and disadvantages that must be evaluated prior to final process selection. Table 3-1 lists typical residence times and operating temperature ranges for the various incineration processes. Classification of waste against the different incineration processes is presented in Table 3-2. The multiple-hearth, fluidized-bed, and liquid-waste incinerators can be operated under normal incineration and in a pyrolysis mode.

Pyrolysis (air-starved) Incineration

Normal incineration requires 40%-100% excess air over the

72

TABLE 3-1.
Operating Parameters for Incineration Process

Process	Temperature Range	Residence Time
Multiple-hearth	600-1,000° F (Drying zone) 1,400-1,800° F (Incineration)	0.25 to 1.5 hr
Fluidized-bed	1,400° F-1,800° F	Liquids and gases—seconds Solids—longer
Liquid incinerator	1,200-3,000° F	0.1-2 s
Direct flame	1,000-1,500° F	0.3-0.5 s
Catalytic combustor	600-1,000° F	1 s
Rotary kiln	(1,500° F max) 1,500-3,000° F	Liquid and gases—seconds Solids—hours
Wet-air oxidation	300-550° F (1,500 psig)	10-30 min
Molten salt	1,500-1,800° F	0.75 s
Multiple chamber	1,500-1,800° F	Gases seconds solids—minutes
Pyrolysis	900-1,500° F	12-15 min

From Hitchcock

TABLE 3-2.
Incinerator/Waste Selection Chart

Waste Type	Rotary Kiln	Multiple Hearth	Fluidized Bed	Liquid Incinerator	Catalytic Combustor	Multiple Chamber Incinerator	Wet-Air Oxidation	Molten-Salt Incinerator
Granular homogeneous		x	x					
Irregular bulky	x							
Low melting point (tar, etc.)	x		x	If material can be pumped		x		
Organic compounds with fusible ash constituents	x	x						
Organic vapor laden				x	x			
High organic strength, toxic				x			x	
Organic liquids				x				x
Waste contains halogenated aromatic compounds (2,200 F)	x		x x	If liquid				x x
Aqueous organic sludges		x					x	

73

stoichiometric value. Pyrolysis is theoretically a zero-air indirect-heat process. However, in practical applications it is an air - starved process in that combustion is occurring with air levels less than stoichometric requirements for combustion. In pyrolysis waste organic compounds are distilled or vaporized to form combustible gas, which is discharged from the furnace. Heat for the process can be provided by the partial combustion of the pyrolysis gas with the furnace and by the combustion of elemental carbon. The unoxidized portion of the combustible gas may be used as fuel in an external combustion chamber, with the resulting energy recovered by conventional-waste-heat-boiler technology. Fixed carbon levels in the furnace ash are higher for pyrolysis than for normal incineration. Pyrolysis is normally employed when the waste material has a high calorific content. Autogenous sludges with a high calorific value (Btu-to-moisture ratio greater than 3,500 Btu/lb of water) are often best processed in oxygen-starved conditions. Normal incineration is used when a specific requirement exists for low level orf fixed carbon in the furnace ash, and when the higher temperatures do not create ash fusion problems.

Multiple-Hearth Furnace

Figure 3-3 shows a multiple-hearth furnace incineration system. Such furnaces range from 6 to 25 ft. dia, 12 to 75 ft.

high. The diameter and number of hearths depends on the waste feed; required processing time, and type of thermal processing employed.

Normal incineration usually requires a minimum of six hearths, while pyrolysis applications require a greater number. Normally sludge or other waste material enters the furnace by dropping through a feed port located in the furnace top. Rabble arms and teeth, attached to a vertically positioned center shaft, rotate counterclockwise to spiral the sludge across the hearths and through the furnace. The waste drops from hearth to hearth through passages alternately located either along the periphery of the hearth or adjacent to the central shaft. Although the rabble arms and teeth all rotate in the same direction, additional agitation of the waste (back rabbing) is accomplished by reversing the angles of the rabble tooth pattern and the rotational speed of the central shaft.

Burners and combustion air ports are located in the walls of the furnace. Each hearth contains temperature sensors and controllers. The hearths are made of refractory, and the central shaft is cast iron and often insulated with castable refractories. The rabble arm and teeth are alloy castings. Materials vary in grade to suit waste requirements.

Cleaning of the multiple-hearth-furnace exhaust gas is usually accomplished by passing the hot gas from the furnace or from

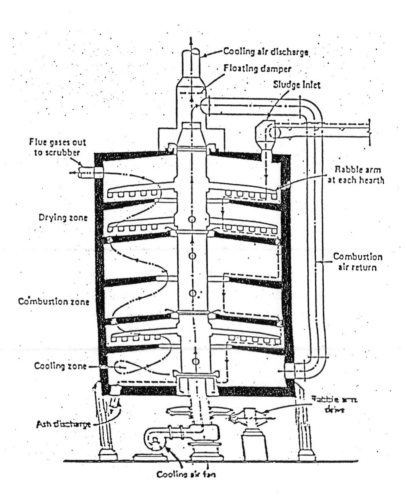

Figure. 3-3 shows multiple-hearth incinerator.

a waste heat reboiler through a precooler, where it is cooled to the adiabatic saturation temperature by spraying fine water droplets into the hot gas stream. Normally the adiabatic saturation temperature ranges from 170° to 190° R, depending on the water vapor content of the gas. The cool gas is then passed through a venturi throat into which additional water is sprayed. A 20- to 35-in. water column pressure-drop in the venturi throat provides the energy needed to collect the fine particulates on the water droplets in the gas stream.

The gas stream with entrained water then enters a particle disengagement unit, if additional cooling is required. The gas is now subcooled (approx. 120° F) and significantly stripped of water vapor, greatly reducing total volume. After passing through an induced draft fan, the effluent gas is discharged to the atmosphere.

Multiple-hearth furnaces operating in pyrolysis or oxygen-starved modes can handle feed materials with heat-release potentials greater than 25,000 Btu/lb of water and still maintain internal temperatures of 1,200° to 1,500° F. Temperatures inside the external combustion chamber can approach up to 3,000° F, greatly increasing the temperature driving force for energy recovery.

Fluidized bed

The fluidized-bed is a simple device consisting of a refractory lined vessel containing inert granular material (see Figure 3-4). Gases are blown through this material at a rate sufficiently high to cause the bed to expand and act as an ideal fluid. The fluidizing gases are injected through nozzles that permit flow up into the bed but restrict downflow of the material. Normally bed design restricts combustion to the immediate area of the bed. This maintains the "free board" area above the bed for separating the inert particles from the rising gases and for minor combustion of devolatilized components.

The hot gases leave the fluidized bed and enter heat-recovery or gas cleaning devices that are similar to those used with multiple hearth furnaces and other incinerators. Sludge of waste feed enters the bed through nozzles located either above or within the bed. Because of the intimate contact between combustion gases and the waste being burned, excess air for normal incineration is usually limited to approximately 40% above the stoichiometric air requirements for combustion of the waste.

Fluidized beds are subject to problems caused by low ash-fusion temperatures. These can be avoided by keeping the operating temperature below the ash fusion level or by adding chemicals that raise the fusion temperature of the ash to an acceptable level.

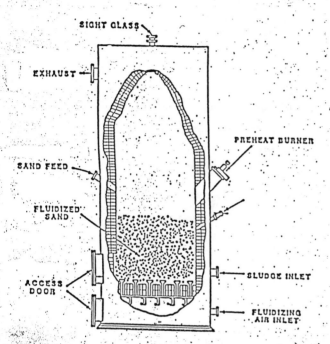

SIGHT GLASS

EXHAUST

SAND FEED

FLUIDIZED SAND

ACCESS DOOR

PREHEAT BURNER

SLUDGE INLET

FLUIDIZING AIR INLET

Figure 3-4. Shows a fluid-bed incinerator

Liquid-Waste Incinerators

The liquid-waste incinerator is probably the most flexible, and certainly the most labor free. Here the feed waste acts as a liquid and exhibits a viscosity less than 10,000 SSU (see Figure 3-5). The heart of the system is a waste atomization device. Because a liquid combustion device is essentially a suspension burner, efficient and complete combustion is obtained only if the waste is adequately divided or atomized and mixed with the oxygen source. Atomization is usually achieved either mechanically using a rotary cup or a pressure atomization system. The burner nozzle is mounted at one end of the refractory-lined chamber and exhaust gases exit from the other end to gas-cleaning equipment. Liquid waste incinerator systems are equipped with waste storage and blending tanks to ensure a reasonably steady and homogeneous waste flow. The tank system is equipped to burn the liquid-waste fumes.

Gas Incinerators

Waste gases are incinetated using direct-flame flare and catalytic combustors. The direct-flame incinerator is effective when the waste gas is not classified as a hazardous waste and has sufficient hydrocarbon content to act as a self supporting fuel requiring only an oxygen source. Flares have reasonable combustion efficiencies. Flares are located on the ground or are

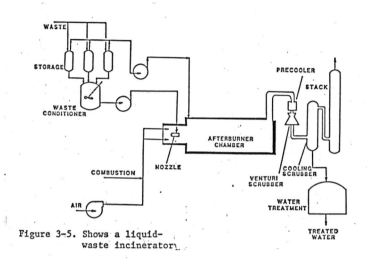

Figure 3-5. Shows a liquid-
waste incinerator.

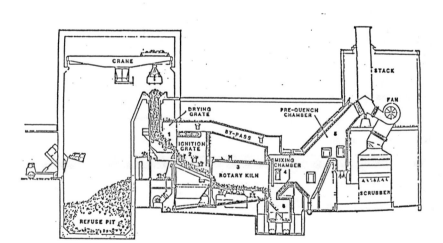

Figure 3-6. Shows a rotary kiln incinerator.

81

elevated. Usually elevated flares are used due to their inherent safety benefits. It is essentially an open pipe through which gases are passed and combusted using ambient oxygen. Steam is often used as an atomization medium to promote complete and smokeless combustion. Pilot burners are normally mounted on the flare for ignigion purpose. These systems are described in detail in the chapter on flares.

Catalytic incinerators are considered for operation with waste containing hydrocarbon levels that are less than 25% of the lower explovosive limit. When the waste gas contains sufficient heating value to cause concern about catalyst burnout, the gas may be diluted by atmospheric air to ensure operating temperatures within the operating limits of the catalyst. However, the waste gas usually contains combustible materials at levels far below those required to support autogenous combustion and usually must be preheated to the catalytic reaction temperatures. Catalytic-combustion systems often produce clean heated gas as product and are well suited for waste heat recovery units. Such units significantly reduce the preheat fuel requirement. In addition to the temperature limitation, catalytic combustion incinerators are also sensitive to poisons, such as heavy metals, phosphates, arsenci compounds, and compounds of halogens and sulfur.

Rotary Kilns

The rotary kiln (Figure 3-6 and 3-7) is a cylindrical, horizontal, refractory-lined shell that is mounted at a slight incline. Rotation of the shell causes mixing of the waste with the combustion air. The length-to-diameter ratio of the combustion chamber normally varies between 2/1 and 10/1, and speed of the rotation is normally in the range of 1 to 5 rpm. Range of combustion temperature is from $1,500°$ to $3,000°$ F. Residence times vary from several seconds to hours, depending on the waste and its characteristics.

Rotary kilns are especially effective when the size or nature of the waste precludes the use of other types of incineration equipment. Special waste materials such as glass bottles, cardboard boxes, discarded packing cases, paper and other unmanageable solid wastes are often co-incinerated in rotary kilns. Kilns can be designed for batch or continuous feeding, which allows for a highly flexible incineration. Continuous feeding is possible if a reasonably no exposed metallic materials of construction, so they resist higher incineration temperatures than others. Temperatures approaching $3,000°$ F, although certainly unusual, are within the capabilities of rotary equipment.

The unit is fired by conventional, as well as liquid-waste burner which enables the installation to double as a liquid-waste incinerator. Waste is delivered to the facility by dump trucks

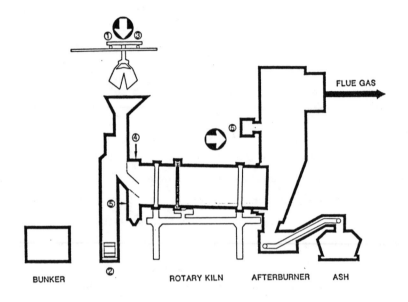

BUNKER   ② ROTARY KILN   AFTERBURNER   ASH

FEED

① SOLID WASTE
② BARREL CHARGING
③ SLUDGE
④ EXHAUST AIR FROM PRODUCTION ROOMS AND TANKS
⑤ FUEL OIL

Figure. 3-7 Typical rotary kiln design.

and deposited in a refuse storage area. The wastes are transfer-red to the shredder by a monorail clamshell and delivered to a ram feeder for introduction to the 1,600° F rotary incinerator. The exhaust gases from the facility pass through an afterburner chamber to ensure complete destruction of organic compounds, and then through a precooler, venturi scrubber, and packed column prior to discharge to the atmosphere.

Wet-Air Oxidation

This process (see Figure 3-8) operates on the principle that the rate of oxidation of organic compounds is significantly increased at higher pressure. Thus, by pressurizing an aqueous orgnic waste (pressures approach 1,500 psi), heating it to an appropriate temperature and then introducing atmospheric oxygen, an incomplete liquid-phase oxidation reaction is produced, which destroys most of the organic compounds. The process exhibits varying levels of combustion efficiency, depending upon the cha-racteristics of the waste. It is often used as a pretreatment step to destroy toxic compounds before conventional biological wastewater treatment. Oxidation efficiency ranges between 600 to 100%. The recovery is done in a countercurrent heat exchanger. The process becomes thermally self-sufficient when the chemical oxygen demand of the influent waste reaches a level of 20,000 to 30,000 mg/L.

85

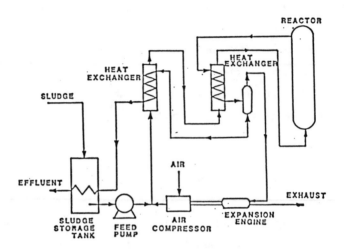

Figure 3-8. Illustrates the wet oxidation process.

Molten-Salt Incinerators

This system is shown in Figure 3-9. Usually a molten-salt bath is composed of approximately 90% Na_2CO_3 and 10% Na_2SO_4 and is designed for operation in the range of 1,500° to 1,800° F. Sometimes K_2CO_3 is used for even lower incineration temperatures. The use of reactive salts, such as eutectic mixtures NaOH-KOH and Li_2CO_3-K_2CO_3 produces the additional benefit of entrapping potentially toxic materials such as heavy metals (i.e., Hg, Pb, Cd, As, Se). This reduces the need of a pollution - control device. The spent salt often can be regenerated or may be land-disposed. Start-up and support fuels include gas, oil, and coal. Waste such as free-flowing powders and shredded materials may be directly fed to molten-salt incinerators. Waste liquids may be sprayed into the combustion air and fed to the unit.

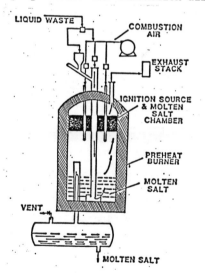

Figure 3-9. Shows features of a molten-salt incinerator.

87

Multiple-Chamber Incinerators

Multiple-chamber incinerators are generally classified as retort types and in-line types. Design aspects of this system are described in the remainder of this chapter.

Ship-Mounted Incinerators

To dispose of organics or organometallics that cannot be burned in conventional incinerators, ship-mounted incinerators are used. However, most of the companies that offer custom incineration are now faced with increasing U.S.EPA scrutiny of their effluents. One viable alternative may be incineration ships that burn hazardous and toxic wastes on the high seas.

Industrial Boilers

Many of the industrial boilers currently burning waste fuels were originally designed for natural gas and/or fuel oil combustion. The most common boiler designs are as follows:

Firetube Boilers - The name firetube boiler is derived from the fact that in boilers of this type heat is transferred from hot combustion products flowing inside tubes to the water surrounding them. Fuel combustion takes place in a cylindrical furnace within the boiler shell. Firetubes run the length of the shell at the sides of, and above, the internal furnace. Gas from the furnace reverses direction in a chamber at the rear and travels forward through the tubes to the front of the boiler. Typical fire tube boiler capacities range from 10,000 to 30,000 lb/hr steam.

Watertube Boilers - Watertube boilers contain thousands of feet of steel tubing (containing water) throughout the combustion chamber. Heat from the combustion products is transferred from the path of the flue gas into the adjacent water tubes. The walls of a watertube boiler are often lined with water tubes to assure minimum heat loss from the boiler shelf. Typical watertube boiler capacities range from 20,000 to 250,000 lb/hr steam.

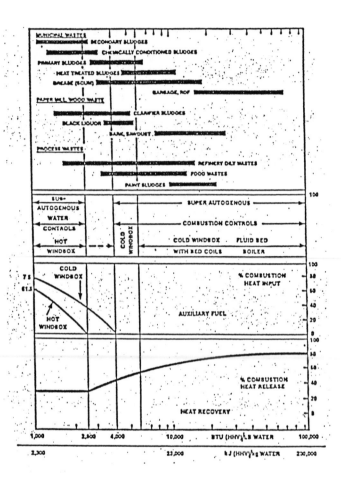

Figure 3-10. Heating values for various wastes.

4.

DESIGN ASPECTS

This chapter deals with specific design aspects of multiple-chamber incinerators for solid waste reduction. In the case of refuse burning, the heterogeneous nature of the materials introduces a complication in that a large number of physical and operating variables exist and can therefore, only be effectively handled on an empirical basis. Theoretical treatment of the complex reactions taking place in some combustion process is, as yet, incomplete, but the empirical art of combustion engineering has developed to an advanced state. The principles of solid-fuel combustion that in general apply to incineration and the basic prospects for combustion efficiency include the following:

- Air and fuel must be in proper proportions.
- Air and fuel especially combustible gases, must be mixed adequately.
- Temperature must be sufficient for ignition of both the solid fuel and the gaseous components.
- Furnace volume must be large enough to provide the retention time needed for complete combustion.
- Furnace proportions must be such that ignition temperatures are maintained and fly-ash entrainment is minizized.

Each of these is discussed in relation to the principal

design components of incinerators.

Ignition Chamber

The ignition mechanism in a refuse-incineration process must be basically one of fuel-bed surface combustion. This is achieved by predominant use of overfire combustion air and minimum use of underfire air. In this context, overfire air is combustion air admitted into the ignition chamber at some point above the pile refuse. Such air is generally furnished through air-supply ports located in, or adjacent to, the charging door on the front wall of the incinerator. Underfirre air is combustion air introduced into the ash pit beneath the fuel bed through airports located on, or adjacent to, the ash pit cleanout doors.

By restricting the introduction of underfire air, relatively low fuel-bed temperatures are maintained, and entrainment of solid particulate matter in the effluent is minimized. If fuel-bed surface combustion through the use of overfire air is to be accomplished, the charging door must be located on the front wall of the ignition chamber or at the end of the chamber farthest from the flame port, because this is where the fresh charge of refuse is introduced. This method of introducing overfire air results in a movement of combustion air concurrent with the travel of the effluent, which has proved to be desirable for efficient combustion.

The emission of solid and liquid particulate materials in combustion effluents from multiple-chamber incinerators is principally a function of the mechanical and chemical processes taking place in the ignition chamber. The fundamental relationships to be considered in evaluating primary-combustion-chamber parameters are length-to-width ratio, arch height, and grate loading. Formulas governing ignition-chamber design are postulated from data obtained from tests of units of varying proportions operated at maximum combustion rate.

Length-to Width-Ratios

In the retort type of multiple-chamber incinerator with rated design capacities of up to 500 lb/hr, satisfactory operating results have been obtained with length-to-width ratios varying from 2.0:1 to 2.5:1. In units with design capacities in excess of 500 lb/hr, optimum results are obtained with a length-to-width ratio of 1.75:1.

Although no sharp distinction has been established, optimum performance for burning rates ranging from 25 to 750 lb/hr has been obtained with the retort type of incinerator. Above this capacity it is difficult to obtain desirable combustion characteristics, proper flame travel, and combustion-air-distribution and still retain the correct relationship of other critical design parameters.

In the in-line type optimum length-to-width ratios commence at 1.65:1 for the 750 lb/hr capacity unit and diminish linearly to 1.1:1 for incinerators with design capacities fo 2,000 lb/hr or more.

Arch Height

Arch height has been observed to have an appreciable affect on contaminant discharges. Incinerators burning similar refuse and with similar grate areas but with different arch heights, have varying combustion rates and contaminant discharge characteristics.

Grate Loading

Acceptable grate loadings range from 15 to 25 $lb/(ft^2)(hr)$ for incinerators with burning rates of 25 to 750 lb/hr. practical consierations for charging and stoking in the smaller incinerators usually results in proportionally larger grate areas and lower grate loadings. For burning rates in excess of 750 lb/hr acceptable grate loadings range from 25 to 35 $lb/(ft^2)(hr)$. A number of refuse incinerators have been designedto operate with grate loadings of 50 to 70 $lb/(ft^2)(hr)$.

Optimum, values of arch heights and grate areas may be estimated from Figures 4-1 and 4-2, respectively, by using the gross heating values of the refuse to be burned and hourly bur-

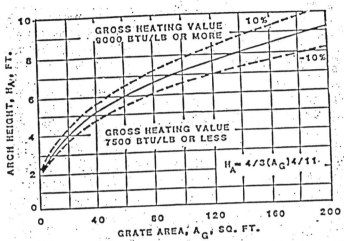

Figure 4-1. Plot of relationship between arc height and grate area for multiple-chamber incinerators.

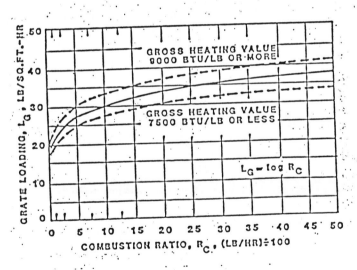

Figure 4-2. plot of relationship between grate loading and combustion rate for multiple-chamber incinerators.

95

ning rates. The curves shown in each plot range over an upper gross heating value of 9,000 Btu/lb or more to a lower gross heating value of 7,500 Btu/lb or less. Interpolation between the upper and lower limits gives the correct arch height and grate area for refuse with a gross heat error beyween these values of + 10%, which is considered to be reasonable. The relationship between arch height to grate area can be calculated from the empirical equation:

$$H_A = 4/3 \ (A_G)^{4/11} \tag{1}$$

where H_A = arch height; defined as the average distance between the top of the grate.

             A_G = grate area or horizontal cross-sectional area of the ignition chamber in square feet.

Secondary Combustion Chamber

The gas-phase or secondary, combustion reactions in a multiple-chamber incinerator are controlled largely by the flame port, mixing chamber, and secondary combustion chamber. The relationship of these parameters is usually determined by certain limiting gas velocities or by the unit volume requirements for the type and quantity of refuse burned. This entails a determination of the combustion-air requirements, weight, and volume of combustion products to be handled, as well as combustion temperatures, heating values, moisture content, percent of combustibles, and ash content.

The primary effect of proper design of the secondary mixing and combustion chambers and ports has improved the combustion of volatile and solid components. The last chamber, or final combustion chamber, is intended to serve a dual purpose-it allows completion of the gas-phase combustion and also serves as a fly-ash settling chamber. The flame port is designed so as to provide a high-gas-velocity zone. Gases leaving the flame port make an abrupt change in the direction and are then expanded in the mixing chamber. The purpose is to promote turbulence and mixing of the effluent from the ignition chamber with secondary combustion air in a high temperature-flame zone.

Optimum design velocities determined for gas flows in the secondary combustion chambers and ports are summarized as follows:

- **Flame port** - Gas velocities at the flameport, or area provided above the bridge wall, should range from 45 to 65 ft/sec.
- **Mixing chamber** - Gas velocities in the mixing chamber may range from 20 to 35 ft/sec.
- **Curtain-wall port** - The gas passage beneath the curtain-wall port should be desinged to give gas velocities ranging from 10 to 15ft/sec.

- **Secondary combustion chamber** - Gas velocities in the secondary combustion chamber should not exceed 10ft/sec.

Combustion Air

The final relationship to be considered in evaluating multiple-chamber design parameters affecting combustion efficiency and contaminant discharge are those of combustion-air supply and distribution, and the requirements for burners to supply auxiliary heat.

Sufficient air must be supplied to the incinerator to allow for the maximum combustion of the oxidizable materials charged and it must be introduced and distributed in such a manner as to reduce discharge contaminants to a minimum. This can be accomplished by the amount of air theoretically required for complete combustion of the refuse. The air supply should be distributed so that not more than 10% of the total volume of air is introduced underfire or beneath the fuel bed. Approximately 70% of the air should be introduced overfire or above the fuel bed and 20% admitted through the secondary air-ports into the mixing chamber. Where excess air is required to control incinerator temperatures, the introduction of this air should be made through additional overfire or secondary air-ports. Secondary combustion air should be provided through controllable air-inlet ports located adjacent to the bridge wall.

It is not unusual for multiple-chamber incinerators to operate in a range of 100%-300% excess combustion air. Air-port areas ordinarily are sized to deliver about 50% of the total air required in the combustion process, that is, theoretical air plus about 100% excess air. The balance of excess air enters as leakage through expansion joints, through the charging door when refuse is introduced, and at other points of air leakage.

Auxiliary Heat

Often the inclusion of burners in the design of a unit is made in anticipation of human error. The use of burners to provide auxiliary heat in multiple-chamber incinerators is normally not required for the burning of Type 1 refuse.

The higher moisture content of Type 2 refuse makes it much more difficult to burn. This often requires the addition of a burner in the ignition chamber as well as a secondary burner in the mixing chamber. The function of a burner is of course to provide auxiliary heat, when and if needed. The higher the moisture content of the refuse, the greater are the auxiliary heat requirements. The determination of the size of burners required should be based on the highest moisture content of refuse expected to be burned in the unit. Auxiliary burners should be fired with either natural gas or manufactured gas.

Stack Draft

The normal method of producing a negative pressure within the ignition chamber is by the use of a natural-draft stack that utilizes the buoyancy of the hot flue gases. Draft produced in this manner is directly related to the height of the stack and to the difference in the reciprocals of the absolute temperature of the flue gas and ambient air. The theoretical draft requirements of a stack can be calculated from the following formula:

$$D_t = 0.52\,PH\left(\frac{1}{T_0} - \frac{1}{T_a}\right) \tag{2}$$

where D_t = theoretical draft in inches of water column
P = barometer pressure (psi)
H = height of the stack above breeching (ft)
T_0 = ambient temperature (°R)
T_a = average stack temperature (°R)

The velocity of the effluent in the stack and the cross-sectional area of the stack affect the usable or available draft. As the velocity within the stack increases or its cross-sectional area decreases, the losses due to friction increase proportionately. This reduces the available draft. Draft losses can be calculated from the following formulas:

$$F_s = \frac{0.008 \cdot HV}{(D)(T)} \tag{3}$$

where F_s = friction loss (in. water column)
H = height of stack above breeching (feet)
V = velocity (ft/sec)
D = stack diameter (ft)
T = temperature ('R)

Frictional losses (rectangular stacks):

$$F_s = \frac{0.002\ HV^2}{(m)(T)} \tag{4}$$

where m = hydraulic radius (ft)

Expansion losses, which are usually negligible, can be estimated from

$$F_\ell = \frac{0.012\ V^2}{T} \tag{5}$$

where F_ℓ = headloss (in. water column)

The draft developed by the stack must be sufficient to overcome frictional losses and leave a net draft available of from 0.005 to 0.10 in. water column negative pressure for the inspiration of combustion air through the primary air-ports. The range of total available stack draft required is from 0.12 in.

101

water column for a 50 lb/hr incinerator to 0.3 in. water column
for a 2,000 lb/hr unit.

Design Calculations

In order to use the design factors given in Table 4-1,
calculations are needed to organize incinerator data into a
usable form. The calculations fall into three general catego-
ries:

- Combustion calculations based on refuse composition,
  assumed air requirements, and estimated heat losses.
- Flow calculations based on the properties of the products
  of combustion and assumed gas temperatures.
- Dimensional calculations based on simple mensuration and
  empirical sizing equations.

  The following assumptions are applied to the design
  Calculations:
- The burning rate and average refuse composition are
  assumed to be constant. The exception occurs when
  extremes in material quality and composition are
  encountered, in which case the most difficult burning
  condition is assumed.
- The average temperature of the combustion products is
  determined through normal heat-balance calculations.
  Heat losses due to radiation, refractory heat storage and

residue heat content may be assumed to average 20% to 30% of the gross heating value of the refuse during the first hour of operation.

- The overall average gas temperature should be about 1,000° F when calculations are based on 300% excess combustion air and the heat-loss assumptions previously given.

- The temperatures used in checking gas flow velocities are approximations of the actual temperature gradient in the incinerator since the products of combustion cool in passing from the flame port to the stack outlet.

- In draft velocities in the combustion air-ports (overfire, underfire, and secondary) are assumed to be equal, with a velocity pressure of 0.1 in. water column (which is equivalent to 1,265 ft/min). Draft systems should be designed in such a way so that the available draft in the primary combustion chamber is about 0.1 in. water column. Oversizing of adjustable air-ports ensure maintenance of proper air induction.

- Air-ports must be sized for admission of theoretical air plus 100% excess air. The remaining air enters the incinerator through the open charging door during batch operation and through expansion joints, cracks around doors, etc. Supplementary computations are usually

103

TABLE 4-I. MULTIPLE-CHAMBER INCINERATOR DESIGN FACTORS

Item and Symbol	Recommended Value
Primary combustion zone:	
Grate loading, L_o	10 log Rc [lb/(hr)](ft²); Rc equals the refuse-combustion rate in lb/hr
Grate area, A_g	Rc ~ Lg (ft²)
Average arch height, H_A	$\beta(Ac)^{4/11}$ (ft)
Length-to-width ratio (approximate): Retort; In line	Up to 500 lb/hr, 2.5:1 to 2:1. Over 500 lb/hr, 1.75:1, diminishing from about 1.7:1 for 750 lb/hr to about 1.2:1 for 2,000-lb/hr capacity. Oversquare acceptable in units of more than 11 ft ignition-chamber length.
Secondary combustion zone:	
Gas velocities:	
Flame port at 1,000°F, V_{FP}	55 ft/sec
Mixing chamber at 1,000°F, V_{MC}	25 ft/sec
Curtain-wall port at 950°F, V_{CWP}	About 0.7 of mixing-chamber velocity
Combustion chamber at 900°F, V_{CC}	5 to 6 ft/sec always less than 10 ft/sec
Mixing-chamber downpass length, L_{MC}, from top of ignition-chamber arch to top of curtain-wall port	Average arch height (ft)
Length-to-width ratios of flow cross sections:	
Retort, mixing chamber, and combustion chamber	Range—1.3:1 to 1.5:1
In line	Fixed by gas velocities due to constant incinerator width
Combustion air:	
Air requirement batch-charging operation	Basic 300% excess air; 50% air requirement admitted through adjustable ports; 50% air requirement met by open charge door and leakage
Combustion-air distribution:	
Overfire-air ports	70% of total air required
Underfire-air ports	10% of total air required
Mixing-chamber air ports	20% of total air required
Port sizing, nominal inlet-velocity pressure	0.1-in. water gage
Air-inlet ports oversize factors:	
Primary air inlet	1.2
Underfire-air inlet	1.5 for over 500 lb/hr to 2.5 for 50 lb/hr
Secondary air inlet	2.0 for over 500 lb/hr to 5.0 for 50 lb/hr
Furnace temperature (average temperature, combustion products):	1,000°F
Auxiliary burners (normal-duty requirements):	
Primary burner	3,000 to 10,000
Secondary burner	4,000 to 12,000 Btu per lb of moisture in the refuse
Draft requirements:	
Theoretical stack draft, D_{Th}	0.15 for 50 lb/hr; 0.30 for 1,000 lb/hr, uniformly increasing between sizes; 0.35 for 2,000 lb/hr
Available primary-air-induction draft, D_A (assume equivalent to inlet-velocity pressure)	0.1-in. water gage
Natural-draft stack velocity, V_s	Less than 30 ft/sec at 900°F

TABLE 4-2.

Chemical Properties and Combustion Data for Paper, Wood, and Garbage

Analysis

Constituent	Sulfite Paper[a]	Average Wood[b]	Douglas Fir	Garbage[d]
Carbon	44.34	49.56	52.30	52.78
Hydrogen	6.27	6.11	6.30	6.27
Nitrogen		0.07	0.10	
Oxygen	48.39	43.83	40.50	39.95
Ash	1.00	0.42	0.80	1.00
Gross heating value[e] (Btu/lb)	7,590	8,517	9,050	8,820

Combustion Data

	Sulfite Paper		Average Wood		Douglas Fir		Garbage	
Constituent[f]	Cubic Feet	Pounds	Cubic Feet	Pounds	Cubic Feet	Pounds	Cubic Feet	Pounds
Theoretical air	67.58	5.165	77.30	5.909	84.16	6.433	85.12	6.507
40% saturation at 60° F	63.05	5.188	77.34	5.935	84.75	6.461	85.72	6.536
Flue gas with theoretical air:								
Carbon dioxide	13.993	1.625	15.641	1.816	16.51	1.917	16.668	1.935
Nitrogen	53.401	3.947	61.104	4.517	66.53	4.918	67.234	4.976
Water formed	11.787	0.560	11.487	0.546	11.84	0.563	11.880	0.564
Water (air)	0.471	0.023	0.539	0.026	0.587	0.028	0.593	0.029
Total	79.652	6.155	88.771	6.905	95.467	7.426	96.375	7.495
Flue gas with percent excess air as indicated:								
0	79.65	6.16	88.77	6.91	95.47	7.43	96.38	7.50
50.0	113.44	8.74	127.42	9.86	137.55	10.64	139.24	10.77
100.0	147.23	11.32	166.07	12.81	179.63	13.86	182.00	14.04
150.0	181.26	13.91	204.99	15.78	222.01	17.09	224.86	17.21
200.0	215.28	16.51	243.91	18.75	264.38	20.12	267.72	20.58
300.0	283.33	21.70	321.75	24.68	349.13	26.58	353.44	27.12

[a] Sulfite-paper constituents:
Cellulose $(C_6H_{10}O_5)$ 84½%
Hemicellulose $(C_5H_{10}O_5)$ 1%
Lignin $(C_4H_{10}O_3)$ 6½%
Resin $(C_4H_{10}O_2)$ 1%
Ash $(C_{20}H_{30}O_3)$ 1%

[b] Kent, R. T., Mechanical Engineers Handbook, 11th ed., Wiley, N.Y. 1936, pp. 6-104.
[c] Kent, R. T., Mechanical Engineers Handbook, 12th ed., Wiley, N.Y. 1950, pp. 2-40.
[d] Estimated.
[e] Dry basis.
[f] Based on 1 lb.

required in determining necessary auxiliary-gas-burner sizes, stack draft control, and auxiliary-fuel-line piping. If the moisture content of refuse is less than 10% by weight, burners usually are not required. A moisture content of 10%-20% normally indicates the necessity for installation of mixing-chamber burners, and a moisture content of more than 20% usually indicates that ignition-chamber burners also must be included.

Gas Scrubbers

Gas Scrubbers employing water sprays are sometimes used in connection with incinerator operations in order to condition the effluent. Their purpose is to cool the effluent to a temperature low enough so that an induced-draft fan may be used to replace a stack or to remove large fly-ash particles. There are several basic considerations that are important in designing a gas scrubber. Perhaps the most important is that htere be no carryover of water in the effluent discharged from the fan. In order to prevent this occurrence the scrubber design should provide sufficient residence tome to completely vaporize the water entrained in the effluent. To accomplish this the water gas mixture should be retained within the scrubber for about 1 to 1 1/2 seconds and velocities should not exceed 15 ft/sec. The design parameters recommended for gas-scrubbers are summarized as follows:

- The water rate to the scrubber should be about 1 GPM for every 100 lb/hr of rated incinerator capacity. This gives a water to gas ratio of about 1 GPM per 400 SCFM of effluent.

- The exhaust fan should be designed to handle 700 CFM at 350° F for every 100 lb/hr incinerator capacity.

- The fan should be designed to provide 0.5 in. static pressure for a 50 lb/hr incinerator, uniformly increasing to 1.5in. for a 2,000 lb/hr incinerator. These static pressures should be developed with the fan operating at 350° F. The static pressure developed by fans operating at 350° F is approximately two-thirds of that developed when handling air at ambient temperatures. When selecting an induced-draft fan from the manufaturer's catalog, one should be chosen that will develop a static pressure 50% higher than those just given, or 3/4 inch for a 50 lb/hr incinerator to 2 1/4 inch for a 2,000 lb/hr incinerator.

- The horsepower requirement of the fan should be based on the full capacity of the fan at ambient temperatures and not at 350° F. .

The internal sizing of chambers and ports in a scrubber can be determined from the data given in Figure 4-4.

Refractory Walls, Linings, and Insulations

The minimum specifications for refractory materials used for lining the exterior walls of multiple-chamber incinerators are the following:

- Type 1 and Type 2 refuse-burning service:
. Firebrick, high heat duty - pyrometric cone equivalent not less than 32.5.
. Castable refractory, not less than 120 lb/ft^3 - pyrometric cone equivalent not less than 17.

- Wood, sawdust, and other high temperature service:
. Firebrick, superduty-pyrometric cone equivalent not less than 24.
. Plastic - pyrometric cone equivalent not less than 34, not less than 130 lb/ft^3

Minimum refractory thickness for lining exterior walls (including arches) of incinerators burning all classes of refuse are the following:

- Up to and including 350 lb/hr capacity:
  Castable refractory or plastic-4 in, firebrick-4 1/2in.
  Above 350 lb/hr capacity: all refractory - 9in.

Stacks should be lined with refractory material with a minimum service temperature of 2,000° F. In low-capacity units the minimum lining thickness should be 2 1/2; in units larger than 350 lb/hr, 4 1/2 in.

Doors should be lined with refractory material with a minimum service temperature of 2,800° F. Units smaller than 100 lb/hr, should have door linings of 2-in. minimum thickness. In the size range of 100 to 350 lb/hr the linings should be increased to 3 inches. In the units with capacities from 350 to 1,000 lb/hr the doors should be lined with 4 inches of refractory. In the units of 1,000 lb/hr and more, linings should be 6 inches.

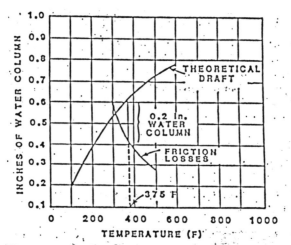

Figure 4-3. Draft at breeching of a multiple-chamber basement installation vs. average stack-gas temperature. Source: Weintraub.

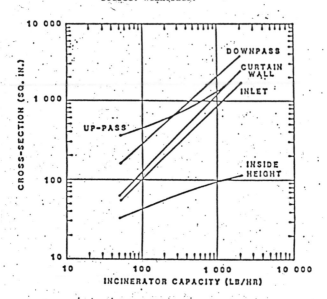

Figure 4-4. Plot for estimating the internal cross-section of scrubbers.

NOTATION

A	percent adhesion	m	hydraulic radius
A_G	grate cross section	N	Avagadro's number
C	slip velocity correction factor	n	particle number concentration
C_D	drag coefficient	q_0	number atoms per unit volume
C_p	specific heat at constant pressure	R'	particle-to-collector-diameter ratio
D	diameter		
D_t	theoretical draft	Re	Reynolds number
d_p	particle diameter	s	average surface roughness
F_{ℓ}	head loss	T	temperature
F_s	friction loss	TA	theoretical air
f	drag force	t	time
g	gravitational acceleration	U	velocity
H	stack height above breeching	u_t	terminal settling velocity
H_A	arch height	V	stack gas velocity
K	Cunningham correction coefficient	V_p	particle volume
		W	mass rate
K_B	agglomeration constant	x	particle displacement

Greek Symbols

η	effective target coefficient	ϱ	fluid density
λ	particle mean free path	ψ	dimensionless impaction parameter
λ'	van der Waals constant		
μ	viscosity		

REFERENCES

American Public Works Association, Public Administration Service, **"Refuse Collection Practice,"** 3rd ed., Washington, DC (1966).

Bradley, R.S., **"The Cohesive Forces Between Solid Surfaces and the Surface Energy of Solids,"** Phil. Mag., 13: 853-862 (1932).

Corn, M., **"The Adhesion of Solid Particles to Solid Surfaces II,"** J.A.P.C.A., 11 (12): 566-584 (Dec. 1961).

Hamaker, H.C., **"The London-van der Waals Attraction Between Spheerical Particles,"** Physica, 4: 1058-1072 (1937).

Whytlaw-Gray, R., and Patterson, H.S., Smoke, Edward Arnold Co., London, 1962.

Weintraub, M., A., Orning, A., and Schwartz, C.R., **"U.S. Bureau of Mines Report,"** INV. 6908 (1967).

Whytlaw-Gray, R., and Patterson, H.S., Smoke, Edward Arnold Co., London, 1962.

Williamson, J.E., MacKnight, R.J., and Chass, R.L., **"Multiple-Chamber incinerator Design Standards,"** Los Angles County Air Pollution Control District (1960).

5.

INCINERATION AND THERMAL TREATMENT TECHNOLOGY

It is estimated that industry now wpends $5 -billion to treat hazardous wastes and that amount is expected to double by 1990, when U.S. plants will be treating some 280 million metric tons per year of waste. Pressures are growing for alternatives to land fills for hazardous wastes handling. The costs of placing wastes in landfills has doubled since 1984 and increasingly stringent regulations and restrictions will make the practice more difficult.

Treatment or Destruction

Destruction and detoxification include a broad range of degrading processes. The basic methods of destruction or detoxification vary widely. Oxidation by a wide variety of technologies is probably the most widely considered degradation or destruction method. **Incineration** is the ultimate in practical oxidation/destruction. Active oxidizing compounds such as ozone or peroxides are also employable where chemicals reaction will take place. More advanced or developmental technologies to promote chemical reactions such as ultra violet energy, high energy radiation are further examples of energy methods.

Nonoxidation methods include chemical reduction; biological methods - aerobic/anaerobic mocrobiological systems as well as

113

macrobiological methods, such as the use of aquatic plants in limited applications. Organic chemicals resisting degradation and destruction are defined as **refractory organics.**

Thermal Destruction

Incineration is a most effective form of managing the disposal of many wastes, such as combustible solids, semi-solids, sludges and concentrated liquid wastes. It reduces, if not eliminates potential environmental risks and potentially converts, wastes into recoverable energy. Comparing incineration to other disposal options, advantages may become evident in specific applications,especially as more wastes become regulated and as added prohibitions and increasingly burdensome costs are placed on land disposal.

Incineration reduces weight and volume to a small fraction of the initial charge, residual ash is sterile, and systems usually require a relatively small operational area. Wastes can often be incinerated on-site and do not have to be transported elsewhere; minimizing potential environmental liabilities. Technology currently exists to destroy even the most hazardous materials in complete and effective manners, and heat recovery techniques are available to offset operating costs in sale or use of energy produced. This latter option is a developing option and will probably evolve in the future as economics dictate.

There are various technologies available in incineration of hazardous wastes. These are summarized in Table 5-1. These incineration systems consist of various components and subsystems. Because of the wide diversity in chemical and physical characteristics of hazardous wastes, a range of techniques have been developed for their disposal. Included in incineration technology are at-sea or ocean incineration possibilities. This latter technology has to-date not received EPA approval. Mobil incineration and incinerators for hazardous and toxic wastes are among operational facilities growing in use and practice.

Emerging technologies in thermal treatment and destruction include: high temperature fluid wall; plasma arc; wet oxidation; and supercritical water. **High temperature fluid wall treatment** is efficient with radiant heat temperatures up to 4000° F. Scale up of cylinder core diameters (above 12 inches) offer difficulty in development due to core thermal stress. **Plasma arc** offers very high energy (up to 50,000° F.) breaks chemical bonds directly, however, low throughout may limit applications. **Wet oxidation** is ideal for aqueous wastes too dilute for incineration. Not applicable to highly chlorinated hydrocarbons, it is commercially used as a pre-treatment to biological destruction. **Supercritical water** is finding some success for destruction of chlorinated aqueous wastes too dilute to incinerate.

Heat or energy recovery possibilities are constantly being

TABLE 5-I. THERMAL TREATMENT METHODS

Process	Description	Wastes Treated
Open burning	Combustion without control of air, containment of reaction, and control of gaseous emissions.	Waste explosives.
Open pit burning	Combustion in a screened pit equipped with air injection nozzles.	Industrial trash, tar sludges,
Incineration	Enclosed device using controlled flame combustion.	
Rotary kiln	Rotating combustion chamber temperatures from 810°C to 1650°C.	Combustible solids, liquids, gases, tars, sludges, waste chemical warfare agents, and munitions.
Fluidized bed	Bed of inert granular material, e.g., sand. Air forced up through bed to make particles act like a fluid. This agitation causes mixture of waste with air and allows larger particles to be burned. Temperatures generally from 760°C to 870°C.	Petroleum and paper industries, sewage sludge.
Multiple hearth	Refractory lined shell with hearths located above one another. Wastes injected at top and fall from one hearth to another. Temperatures from 315°C to 980°C.	Sewage sludge, tars, solids, gases.
Liquid injection	Vertical or horizontal units into which atomized waste is sprayed. Temperatures from 650°C to 1650°C.	Combustible liquid wastes, e.g., chlorinated hydrocarbons.
High temperature processing	Heat and/or pressure used to destroy or alter waste.	
Calcination	Thermal decomposition used to drive off volatiles and leave a dry powder.	Carbonates, hydroxides, sulfites, sulfides.
Wet oxidation	Solids solubilized and oxidized under high pressure.	Sewage sludge.
Pyrolysis	Destructive distillation in absence of oxygen. Wastes broken down into solid, liquid, and gaseous components.	

116

explored in the incineration of hazardous organic wastes. One such process is being developed by The John Zink Co., as shown in Figure5-1, which is a schematic of a test series with the Hazardous Waste Steam Generator. It consists of a radiation section fitted with a YE-O type burner, thermal oxidizer, fire tube boiler and vent stack. A thermal oxidizer is incorporated between the radiation section and the fire tube boiler.

Another commercially available hazardous waste incinerator is designed and available from Hirt Combustion Engineers. Liquid wastes can be oxidized easily if they have a viscosity of at least 200 SSU and can pass through a 30-mesh strainer. If liquids do not possess these characteristics, special arrangements can be made to introduce them into the burners. After the combustion process, any particulates in the exhaust gas are removed by a hot temperature baghouse, and any chlorine, fluorine, and sulfur are removed by a scrubber. Fuel economy is achieved by heat recovery in waste heat boilers with economizers and air preheaters. This reduces the operating expense for fuel to a minimum. These and similar units have to pass the toughest regulatory requirements.

Other commercially available units include a 2-foot diameter mobile demonstration unit fluidized bed combustion unit for hazardous and toxic waste destruction. This Waste-Tech services Inc. unit has proven sucessful in safely destroying a wide variety of

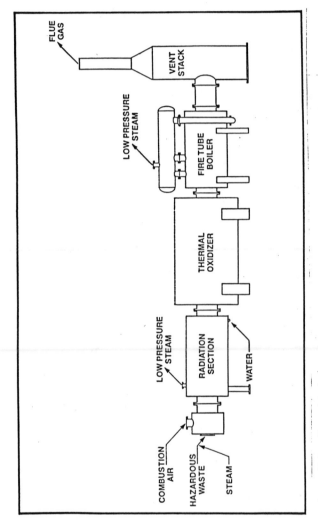

Figure 5-1. Hazardous waste steam generator.
(courtesy: John Zink co.)

hazardous wastes in solid, liquid, slurry and gaseous form. The equipment is also designed to destroy or decontaminate waste materials containing PCB's and dioxins.

Thermal destruction can be effected with oxygen (incineration or combustion) or in the absence of oxygen (pyrolysis). The combustion / incineration process of organics will produce water-carbon dioxide/ash. The presence of halogens, sulfur, phosphorous will produce acid gases depending on the hazardous waste composition. Table 5-2 summarizes some innovative thermal treatment processes coming onto the market.

Incineration - is combustion of wastes by various techniques and may be effected by equipment utilizing horizontal or vertical refractory lined combustion chambers or in a fluidized bed; or molten salts bed. Typical combustion temperatures range from 800 - 3000° F; with residence times from 0.5 to 2.0 seconds. Significant volume and weight reduction of wastes as well as ability to handle a large variety of wastes are the distinct advantage. This technology must be controlled and monitored for air emissions and usually require addition of air pollution control equipment.

Pyrolysis - thermal decomposition in the absence of oxygen breaks down organic wastes in simpler molecules or smaller molecular weights which can be recovered by such methods as condensation or can be more easily combusted than the initial waste.

119

TABLE 5-2. INNOVATIVE THERMAL TREATMENT PROCESSES

Fluidized Bed Incineration – turbulent bed of inert granular matmaterials improve heat transfer to waste streams to be incinerated. These systems usually offer compact designs; simple operation and combine combustion with pollution control.

Wet Oxidation – aqueous media oxidizes suspended and dissolved organics in aqueous waste streams. A reported drawback is in halogenated organics treatment. Supercritical Water Oxidation Process is included in this category.

Molten Salt – waste materials are injected below a bed of molten sodium carbonate for incineration. The molten salt bed requires a lower temperature than for waste combustion and the bed acts as a scrubbing medium for acid gases.

Chemical Transformation – chemical reactions transform a waste into less toxic materials. Catalytic dehalogenation is an example of this technology; the process is not a destruction method.

Molten Glass – organics are destroyed in a pool of molten glass as the heat transfer medium. The molten bed entraps ash and inorganics and the resulting residue is a nonleachable glass.

Plasma Systems – use extremely high temperature gases in the plasma state for waste destruction. Plasma gases can reach 10,000 deg. F which are highly destructive to molecular composit-ions.

Electric Reactors – pyrolysis of a waste stream (e.g., granular solids) by radiant heat in an electrically heated fluidd wall re-actor. Temperatures can typically reach 4000 deg. F.

Temperatures are such that will cause a breaking of carbon to carbon bonds in organics and typically are less than 1000° F. Possibility of by-product or fuel recovery is a distinct advantage which can be used as supplementary energy as well as possibilities for reduced air emissions. Some organizations involved in this development include Midland-Rose Co. (Continuous and Batch - Pyrotherm), Russell and Axon (high temperature pyrolysis with oxygen).

Supercritical Water Process - uses a high pressure reactor for organic wastes oxidation. Liquid water at 705°F acts as a decomposing media and solvent where aqueous solutions at such temperature and under high pressure destroys wastes at high efficiency.

Electric Reactors - also known as **high temperature fluid wall** reactors in which liquid or granular hazardous wastes may be pyrolyzed by 4000° F radiant heat. The reactor is a tubular refractory core emitting heat supplied by electrical elements in the reactor jacket. An inert gas is injected during the process to coat the reactor walls to protect them from the high temperatures. This is clearly one of the emerging technologies being studied for hazardous wastes destruction. Thagard Research Corp. (high temperature fluid wall HTFR); and J.M. Huber Co. (advanced electrical reactor) are among companies developing this technology.

121

Plasma Arc - Wastes are pyrolyzed yielding combustible gases by exposure to a gas energized to a plasma state by electric discharge. Plasma gases can reach temperatures which can be extremely destructive to molecular composition of wastes. Destruction of hazardous wastes uses high temperature gas or a mixture of gases that can include ambient air bringing about chemical changes. Plasma is produced by heating gas or gas mixtures to temperatures as high as 9-10,000° F by passing the gas through or along an electric arc between electrodes in a plasma generator.

Plasma Technology Developments

Plasma technology which has been around since the early part of this century is beginning to be applied to hazardous wastes destruction. Plasma technology equipment and systems supplies are finding applications and designing systems for the destruction of hazardous wastes. Examples include chlorinated organics such as polychlorinated biphenyls which can be broken down into carbon monoxide, carbon dioxide, monatomic chlorine, hydrogen, oxygen, and nitrogen. Exit gases can then be fed to a scrubber removing particulate and HCl; off-gases from the scrubber can be flared or recycled to the system for use as a fuel.

Examples of a hazardous waste destruction plasma systems include the Pyrolysis System Co. (Welland, Ont.) which is supported by the N.Y. State Dept. of Environmental Conservation and EPA. Plasma-generating equipment for tests and demonstration is available from Westinghouse Waste Technologies Services Division (Madison, PA). Plasma Energy Corp. (Raleigh, NC) is testing and demonstrating plasma systems. SKF Steel Engineering Co. (Hofore, Sweden) has designed and built a 0.5 ton per hour wastes destruction plant.

On-Site Incineration - Case History

A permit to burn PCBs has been issued to GA Technologies (San Diego, CA) by the USEPA. Issued under the Toxic Substances Control Act (TSCA), the permit allows to use a transportable circulating bed incinerator to burn PCBs (polychlorinated biphenyles) anywhere in the nation.

The totally enclosed design features a circulating bed combustion process minimizing the potential for exposure to workers and population at large. The on-site treatment capability of the unit virtually elimintaes potential risk of a spill of PCB material during transportation.

As early as 1979, EPA estimated that there were 750-million pounds of PCB material in use in the U.S., with an additional 20-million pounds of waste awaiting safe treatment and/or disposal. This waste backlog has increased substantially since then, partially due to stricter regulations that have been adopted.

Destroying the wastes at the place of origin, instead of transporting to an off-site disposal facility will reduce accidental spills and other transportation losses.

Waste Oils/Solvents Disposal

Waste oils and contaminated solvents can be examined as potential fuels for industrial boilers. The term "waste oil" refers to used motor vehicle crank case oils and spent machinery lubricating oils. The quantity of waste oil generated in the United States is estimated to be 1.1 billion gallons per year of which approximately 40 percent is currently burned as a fuel. Additives in such oils include barium, magnesium, zinc, sulfur, nitrogen, calcium, and phosphorous. During use, lubricating oils may also become contaminated from both internal and external sources. For example, when leaded gasoline is used in an automotive engine, the crankcase oil becomes contaminated with lead via the piston rings and cylinder walls (external). Lead alloys are also used as bearing material inside many engine crankcases (internal). The moving parts of machinery or engines also wear, causing internal oil contamination with metals such as iron, chromium, nickel, molybdenum, aluminum, zinc, and magnesium. Environmental impacts of the disposal of waste oils has recently become an area of growing concern. Several studies conducted by State and Federal agencies have documented the presence of contaminants such as chlorinated hydrocarbons and the above-mentioned metals in samples of used motor oils.

The term "spent solvent" refers to a broad classification of waste liquid hydrocarbons. Such solvents are used by a wide variety of industries. They are used in chemical and pharmaceutical processes including reactions, extractions, degreasing, or cleaning operations. Many spent or contaminated solvents are recovered by filtration and distillation or other means to purify the material. However, often the solvent may become contaminated with organic residues or other solvents that render it difficult or too expensive to recover. Generally only non-halogenated solvents are suitable as waste fuels for industrial boilers. Concentrated halogenated solvents are generally poor fuels and their high halogen content render them illegal to burn without acid gas scrubbers. Table 5-3 shows examples of typical solvents used in industry which may be suitable as boiler waste fuels.

Market Needs

Even before the passage of the Resource Conservation and Recovery Act (RCRA) in 1976, hazardous and toxic wastes were generally disposed of by incineration as well as secured landfills and other means considered environmentally sound at the time. As incineration technology has developed in the last decade, a distinction between incinerators used for hazardous or

125

TABLE 5-3. TYPICAL SOLVENTS SUITABLE FOR WASTE FUEL BLENDING *

Ethyl Acetate	Cyclohexane
Acetone	Diethylaniline
Methanol	Diethylamine
Ethyl Ether	Methyl Vinyl Ketone
Toluene	Butanol
Hexane	Dimethoxy Propane
Heptane	Acetic Acid
Isobutyraldehyde	Tetrahydrofuran
Methyl Formate	Methyl Benzyl Ether
Ethanol	Benzyl Alcohol
Propionic Acid	Dibenzyl Ether
Propionic Anhydride	Acetic Anhydride
Methyl Ethyl Ketone	Cyclohexyl Acetate
Dimethylaniline	Triethylamine
Isopropanol	Cyclohexylethylamine
Dimethylformamide	Cyclohexenylethylamine
Tetrahydrofuran	Benzaldehyde
Butenediol	Benzylamine
Xylene	Acetonitrile
Pyridine	Butenol
Ethyl Butenol	Butyl Acetate
Methyl Acetate	Methyl Isobutyl Ketone
3-Hexynol	Isopropyl Acetate
Aniline	Ethyl Benzene
Alcohol 2B	Dimethyl Malonate
Isopropyl Ether	Monobenzylamine

* It should be noted that specific states may not allow carcinogenic
or suspect carcinogenic solvents to be burned in industrial boilers.

nonhazardous wastes has become recognized. Specific applications have reflected the needs for special operating conditions and equipment designs such as 1200 C combustion temperatures; two-second residence times; 3 percent excess oxygen for combustion of highly toxic/thermally stable polychlorinated biphenyls (PCBs). Such conditions have even been spelled out in regulations as the Toxic Substances Control Act (TSCA) of 1976 and RCRA. In 1978 RCRA more fully defined hazardous wastes in relation to incinerator performance and operating conditions for destruction. In 1981 incinerator regulations altered incinerator operational and performance requirements but did add the need for air pollution control devices to be part of the systems.

Both manufacturers and purchasers of such systems have to make complex decisions involving performance, operations and economics about incineration. Equipment available from vendors, manufacturers, and engineering design organization vary over a wide range from boilers only to inclusion of air pollution control devices; energy recovery options to turnkey operation. Some firms will even offer to operate and maintain complete incineration facilities on a contact basis.

Design Requirements

Because complex considerations are associated with design of hazardous waste incinerators, it is important to have an understanding of the factors involve. high to have an understanding of the factors involved. High combustion temperature; extended residence time at high temperature are readily recognized as important but are not the only elements. Combustion chamber design affording turbulent mixing for unburned/hot/oxygen rich combustion gases and maximum combustion reaction rates under flameless conditions are also critically important. Reaction rates under flameless conditions outside the flame envelope are slower and involve different thermal oxidation reaction mechanisms. Thus, hazardous waste incineration design must incorporate and take into consideration the importance of both turbulent mixing and adequate flame contact.

Besides considering mixing and flame contact, other important thermal oxidation mechanisms include: (1) atomized liquid droplet size and evaporation rates; (2) particulate melting and vaporization rates; and (3) adsorption of uncombusted substances on particulate. These rate processes translate into important, practical considerations when designing a hazardous waste incinerator.

Still other factors to consider about waste incineration include:

1. Analysis of the waste (heat of combustion, viscosity, the constituents chemical analysis).

2. The proposed incineration system-its capabilities, design,

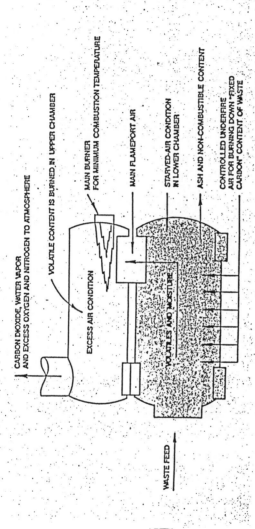

CARBON DIOXIDE, WATER VAPOR
AND EXCESS OXYGEN AND NITROGEN TO ATMOSPHERE

VOLATILE CONTENT IS BURNED IN UPPER CHAMBER

MAIN BURNER
FOR MINIMUM COMBUSTION TEMPERATURE

MAIN FLAMEPORT AIR

STARVED-AIR CONDITION
IN LOWER CHAMBER

ASH AND NON-COMBUSTIBLE CONTENT

CONTROLLED UNDERFIRE
AIR FOR BURNING DOWN "FIXED
CARBON" CONTENT OF WASTE

EXCESS AIR CONDITION

VOLATILES AND MOISTURE

WASTE FEED

Figure 5-2. The principle of controlled-air incineration involves two sequential combustion operations carried out in two separate chambers. (Courtest Ecolaire Combustion Products, Inc.)

129

and materials of construction.

3. Burn schedules-waste loads and feed rates.

4. Emission control equipment and operating conditions.

5. Backup procedures and controls for waste shutoff and/or incinerator shutdown should equipment malfunction or wastes vary beyond intended feed composition.

Burn Data/Analytical Requirements/Monitoring

The following factors should be considered as part of the data requirements and analysis for incinerator operation:

1. Hydrocarbon (HC) and other (chlorine, phosphorous, sulfur, etc.) constituents in waste feed.

2. Exhaust gas emissions and hazardous combustion by-products.

3. Analysis of scrubber water; ash or other residues.

4. Mass and material balances.

5. Removal efficiency of air pollution controls.

6. Average, maximum and minimum temperatures measurement and air feed rates.

7. Continuous measurement may be required for carbon monoxide (CO) and HC in exhaust gases.

This and other data may be required for certification as well as evidence of legal compliance.

Monitoring requirements for permitted incinerator during normal operation may require limits for waste feed rate; CO exhaust gas concentration; combustion temperatures and air fed rates. Particulate emission limitations and performance standards will have to be met (typically particulate matter should not exceed 0.08 gr/dscf when corrected to 12 percent CO_2). To meet regulatory emission requirements consistently, careful waste characterization; feed control; preconditioning flue gases and optimal gas cleaning and mist elimination systems are required.

Test burns of the waste may be desirable to initially develop air pollution designs for specific applications. This is particularly true if the wastes contain organic phosphorus, metal or inorganic salts. Incinerators burning hazardous wastes containing more than 0.5 percent chlorine must remove 99 percent HCl from the exhaust gas. Incinerators processing organic chlorine compounds more than 5-10 percent by weight, using traditional equipment (venturi scrubbers, tray towers, packed beds) should be able to economically meet most required air pollution emission standards.

Incineration at Sea

Twelve years after the first burns in U.S. waters, ocean incineration of hazardous wastes is not a commercial reality in this country. A decade ago, incineration at sea seemed the answer to destroying liquid hazardous wastes. When compared with land-based units, threats to human health were to be limited by

131

a ship's remoteness from people. The ocean's ability to buffer acidic exhaust gases would eliminate the need for costly scrubbers. Little opposition was expected to the "not in my backyard" syndrome that haunts attempts to site waste treatment facilities on land. Opposition however, has been fierce. Three years ago permits to burn 80-million gal of organic compounds in the Gulf of Mexico had raised outcries causing EPA to back off. A similar experience was witnessed late lasy year in new Jersey. If an ocean incineration program is to be developed in the U.S., Congress will likely need to play a major role. New laws may be required to clarify or augment present authority for regulating at-sea incineration, or provide an interim program as better waste-management methods are developed. A recent report "Ocean Incineration: Its role in Managing hazardous Waste," Stock number 05200301046-1, is available for $11 from the Superintendent of Documents, U.S. Government Printing Office, Washington, DC 20402 for those readers wishing a more complete update on this subject.

Process and Equipment Availability

There is a wide array of incineration technologies available for hazardous materials disposed as summarized in Table5-4. The variations and ultimate selection will differ from one application to another depending on:

- Material handling,

TABLE 5-4. INCINERATION TECHNOLOGIES FOR SLUDGES & HAZARDOUS MATERIAL!

Incinerator Type	Design Features and Limitations
Liquid Injection Incineration: Can be designed to burn a wide range of pumpable waste. Also used in conjunction with other incinerator systems as a secondary afterburner for combustion of volatiles. Hot refractory minimizes cool boundary layer at walls. HCl recovery possible.	Limited to destruction of pumpable waste of viscosity of less than 10,000 SS. Usually designed to burn specific waste streams. Smaller units can have problems with clogging of injection nozzles. Probably the most widely used design.
Rotary Kilns: Can accommodate great variety of waste feeds: solids sludges, liquids, some bulk waste contained in fiber drums. Rotation of combustion chamber enhances mixing of waste by exposing fresh surfaces for oxidation.	Rotary kilns are expensive but have economy of scale.
Cement Kilns: Attractive for destruction of harder-to-burn waste, due to very high residence times, good mixing, and high temperatures. Alkaline environment neutralizes chlorine.	Burning of chlorinated waste limited by operating requirments, and appears to increase particule generation.
Boilers (usually a liquid injection design): Energy value recovery, fuel conservation. Availability on sites of waste generators reduces spill risks during hauling.	Cool gas layer at walls result from heat removal. This constrains design to high-efficiency combustion within the flame zone. Nozzle maintenance and waste feed stability can be critical. Where HCl is recovered, high temperatures must be avoided.
Multiple Hearth: Passage of waste onto progressively hotter hearths can provide for long residence times for sludges. Design provides good fuel efficiency. Able to handle wide variety of sludges.	Tiered hearths usually have some relatively cold spots which inhibit even and complete combustion. Opportunity for some gas to short circuit and escape without adequate residence time. Not suitable for waste streams which produce fusible ash when combusted; units have high maintenance requirements due to moving parts in high-temperature zone.
Fluidized-bed Incinerators: Turbulence of bed enhances uniform heat transfer and combustion of waste. Mass of bed is large relative to the mass of injected waste.	Large economy of scale.
At-Sea Incineration: Shipboard (usually liquid injection incinerator): Minimum scrubbing of exhaust gases required by regulations on assumption that ocean water provides sufficient neutralization and dilution. This could provide economic advantages over land-based incineration methods. Also, incineration occurs away from human populations. Shipboard incinerators have greater combustion rates.	Not suitable for waste that are shock sensitive, capable of spontaneous combustion, or chemically or thermally unstable due to the extra handling and hazard of shipboard environment.
Pyrolysis: Air pollution control needs minimum: air-starved combustion avoids volatilization of any inorganic compounds. These and heavy metals go into insoluble solid char. Potentially high capacity.	Some wastes produce a tar which is hard to dispose of. Potentially high fuel maintenance costs.

- Feed system,

- Combustion retention time,

- Secondary oxidation,

- Instrumentation,

- Heat exchangers,

- Energy recovery,

- Pollution control, and

- Residue handling.

Some of the many emerging and developing thermal technologies are described in Table 5-2. Services may range from process, component, and systems design to turnkey operation and facilities maintenance. The many figures included in this article illustrate only some of the wide variety of equipment and applications available. Manufacturers are pursuing many courses of action in response to market needs and regulatory requirements.

TABLE 5-5. EMERGING THERMAL TECHNOLOGIES

Technology	Limitations To Date
Molten Salt: Molten salts act as catalysts and efficient heat transfer medium. Self-sustaining for some wastes. Reduces energy use and reduces maintenance costs. Units are compact; potentially portable. Minimal air pollution control needs; some combustion products, e.g., ash and acidic gases are retained in the melt.	Commercial-scale applications face potential problems with regeneration or disposal of ash-contaminated salt. Not suitable for high ash wastes. Chamber corrosion can be a problem.
High-Temperature Fluid Wall: Waste is efficiently destroyed as it passes through cylinder and is exposed to radiant heat temperatures of about 4,000 F. Cylinder is electrically heated; heat is transferred to waste through inert gas blanket, which protects cylinder wall. Mobile units possible.	To date, core diameters 3, 6, and 12, and cylinder length 172, limit throughput capacity. Scale-up may be difficult due to thermal stress on core. Potentially high costs for electrical heating.
Plasma Arc: Very high energy radiation breaks chemical bonds directly, without series of chemical reactions. Simple operation, very low energy costs, mobile units planned.	Limited throughput. High use of NaOH for scrubbers.
Wet Oxidation: Applicable to aqueous waste too dilute for incineration and too toxic for biological tratment. Lower temperatures required, and energy released by some wastes can produce self-sustaining reaction. No air emissions.	Not applicable to highly chlorinated organics, and some wastes need further treatment. Used as pretreatment to biological wastewater treatment.
Super Critical Water: Applicable to chlorinated aqueous waste which are too dilute to incinerate. Takes advantage of excellent solvent properties of water above critical point for organic compounds. Injected oxygen decomposes smaller organic molecules to CO_2 and water. No air emissions.	Probable high economy of scale. Energy needs may increase on scale-up.

135

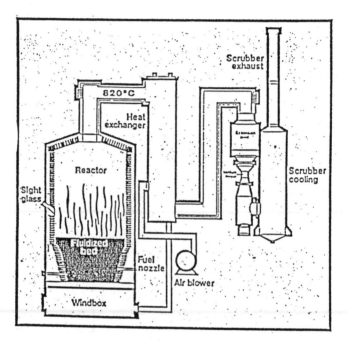

Figure 5-3. Fluidized bed system.

6.

Flare Gas Control

Direct discharge of waste or excess vapors to the atmosphere is unacceptable either because of restrictions imposed by local ordinances or plant practices; concentrations of the contaminants at ground or adjacent platform levels exceed permissible explosion or toxicological threshold limits; and / or metrorological conditions which promote high background concentrations of discharges. Nonhazardous vapors such as waste or low pressure steam are usually discharged directly to the atmosphere. In contrast, hydrocarbon vapors which are discharged on a continuous basis (for example, off-spec product or bypass streams generated during start - up) or intermittently and which cannot be directly discharged to the atmosphere must be disposed of through a closed system and burned in a flare.

The operation of gas flaring is aimed at converting flammable, toxic or corrosive vapors to either nontoxic emissions or to acceptable concentrations by means of combustion. Because flaring is an integral part of petroleum and petrochemical plant operations discussed on this subject are warranted. This chapter covers basic considerations for the planning and design of flaring systems. Included are criteria for establishing safety facilities aimed at preventing overpressuring during the discharge of vapors and liquids. Among the standard pressure - relieving devices described are safety and relief valves, rupture disks, pressure control valves, and equipment blow down valves.

Overview of Flaring

Flare systems are broadly categorized as elevated and ground-level designs. In elevated systems, combustion takes place at the discharge of a stack through a burner and igniter. Ground level flares are more elaborate in design, with basically three types of configurations. One arrangement uses a water spray to disperse the combustion gases; the venturi type takes advantage of the waste streams's kinetic energy to inspirate and mix combustion air with the gas; and finally, multi-jet designs distribute the gas through a cluster of burners.

Figure 6-1 illustrates the features of both elevated and ground level systems. In the elevated system (Figure 6-1A), the relieving gases are sent through an elevated stack from a closed collection system and burned off at the top. The generated flame is open in this case. Figure 6-1B illustrates a ground flare system, where principal components are a knock-out drum, multi-jet burners, a refractory lined rectangular flare box, and a seal drum. The flare flame is returned inside the flare chamber.

Designs often include several pilot burners which burn continuously. Systems must be continuously purged with an inert gas such as nitrogen or with natural gas to maintain an routed back

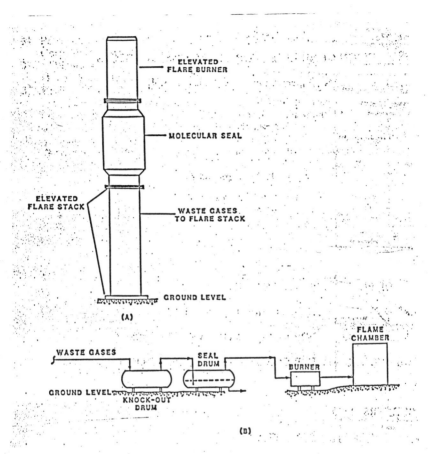

Figure 6-1(A). Elevated flare system; (B) ground level flare system.

to a low pressure process stream, to a fuel system, or to an incineration.

The major components of all flare systems are the relief, safety and depressuring valves; pressure relieving header(s) which convey discharges from safety and pressure control valves in the process unit to the flare; the knock-out drum located ahead of the flare stack; and the flare stack itself which consists of the riser structure, molecular seal, and burner tip.

The riser structure consists of two or more sections; the flare header enters at the bottom section which serves as a flare stack knock-out drum. Condensate carried over from the main knock-out drum is collected in the riser section.

The molecular seal is welded to the riser section. It provides a seal against air entering into the flare stack and minimizes the formation of explosive mixtures in the system. It resembles a bubble cap and creates a seal by taking advantage of the buoyancy of the purge gas to create a zone where the pressure exceeds atmospheric conditions.

The burner tip is a complete assembly which is connected to the molecular seal outlet. Accessories on the burner tips include about three or four gas pilots, a similar number of pilot gas/air mixture assemblies, and steam supply nozzles for steam injection.

Figure 6-2 shows a schematic diagram of the entire flare

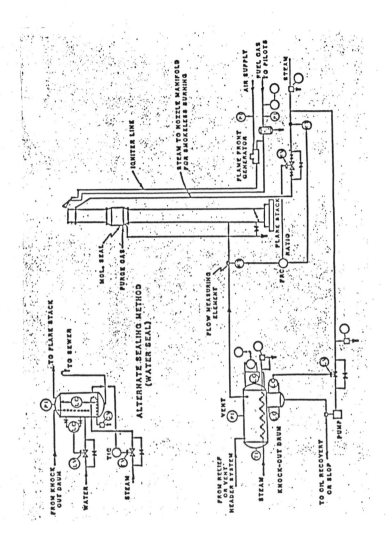

Figure 6-2. Schematic of typical flare gas system (adapted from API, RP 521)

system. The relieving gases from safety relief valves are collected in a horizontal or vertical knock-out drum through a main
header. Condensate carried in the gas is removed at this point.
A constant liquid level is maintained in the boot of the drum.
The liquid is pumped to a slop tank or reused in oil recovery
facilities. Steam is normally used for winterizing. The gas
from the knock-out drum is then sent to an elevated flare stack.
At the bottom of the stack a seal of liquid is maintained.

The stack, comprised of a riser section, molecular seal, and
burner tip, is automatically ignited through the line. A steam
connection is provided for smokeless flares along with a purge
gas connection for maintaining an air-free system. The latter
prevents flashback by maintaining the pressure at the molecular
seal in excess of the atmosphere.

Note that a flame is referred to as being luminous when
incandescent carbon particles are present. When these particles
cool down, smoke is formed. Smoke formation mainly occurs in
fuel-rich systems where a low hydrogen-atom concentration sup-
presses the smoke. Prevention of smoke in flares is normally
accomplished by:

- By the addition of steam.
- By preparing a premixture of fuel and air before
  combustion (this provides sufficient oxygen levels for
  efficient combustion)

- By distribution of the flow of raw gases through a number of small burners.

Steam addition is most commonly used to generate a smokeless flare for economy and superior performance. In steam addition, the raw gas is preheated before entering the combustion zone. If the temperature is high enough, cracking of hydrocarbons occurs. This produces free hydrogen and carbon. When the cracked hydrocarbons enter the combustion zone, hydrogen reacts much faster than carbon. Unless the carbon particles are burned away, they cool down, thus forming smoke. Consequently, to prevent smoke, both hydrogen and carbon or sufficient oxygen must be provided for complete combustion. When steam is added, the hydrogen molecules also tend to separate which minimizes polymerization reactions and forms oxygen compounds which burn at a reduced rate and temperature. The net effect is to prevent cracking. Another explanation for the improved efficiency with steam addition is that the steam reacts with carbon particles forming carbon monoxide, carbon dioxide, and hydrogen, thereby removing the carbon which forms smoke after cooling.

CAUSES AND PREVENTION OF OVERPRESSURE

The initial design stage involves analysis of potential cases leading to discharges from pressure relief valves (i.e., establishing the maximum loading for emergency operations). The maximum load is composed of the individual contributions from the entire process. A conservative design is one which assumes that all contributions are relieving simultaneously under emergency conditions.

It is preferable that relieving overpressures to the flare systems via the pressure relief valves be kept to a minimum, since these valves often do not reseat themselves. This leads to leakage, and consequently, reduced recovery of products. For minor operational upsets, overriding pressure control valves (PCV) strategically located on equipment are incorporated in the control strategy. Examples of such locations are the suction sides of compressors, overhead product lines of fractionating columns, at the beginning or at the end of a series of high pressure reactors, etc. The set point of the PVC is positioned above the operating pressure but below the set-point of the pressure relief valve. They are sized to handle about 40% to 100% of the flow of the safety valves. For about 90% of the emergency operations the system is depressurized through these valves so as to keep to operation of the pressure relief valves to a minimum. Besides overriding pressure control valves, other remotely controlled valves (e.g., motor operated or solenoid operated valves) are also used.

Pressure vessels, heat exchangers, operating equipment, and piping are designed for a specified system pressure. This maximum allowable working pressure is about 10% higher than the normal operating pressure. Pressure relief valves are normally set at or below the maximum allowable working pressure in order to protect equipment. The relieving rate of a pressure relief valve depends upon the cause of system overpressure; principal ones being operational failures and plant fires (API).

Examples of operational failures are closed outlets on vessels, inadvertent valve opening, utility failure, and a variety of miscellaneous actions. In the case of an inadvertent closure of a block valve the pressure in a vessel can exceed the maximum allowable pressure. A pressure relief valve protects the vessel under this situation. If two vessels are in series and isolated by individual block valves, then each vessel must be protected by an individual pressure relief valve. Omission of the block valve in between the vessels or locking the same valve in the open position results in a common system. This arrangement may be protected by a single pressure relief valve. As in the case of block valves, each control valve should be considered as subject to inadvertent operation causing overpressure in the upstream section.

Another common error is the inadvertent opening of a valve from a higher pressure source (e.g., high pressure steam or process fluids connected to a low pressure system). This causes an overpressure exceeding the maximum allowable working pressure.

145

If the block valve is intended for isolation only and normally remains closed, a pressure relief valve may be avoided by locking or sealing the same block valve.

Examples of miscellaneous actions/conditions leading to operational failures are:

- **Reflux failure of a fractionating column** - which can cause flooding of condensers resulting in an overpressure.

- **Heat Exchanger tube failure** - when tube side pressure of an exchanger is much lower than the shell side, rupture of a tube can result from overpressure of the tube side.

- **Internal explosion** - a situation which is not predictable for conventional refinery installations. For some chemical reactions, it is possible to predict the probability of an explosion, in which case, special rupture disks are installed for quick disposal of vapors.

- **Chemical reaction** - where vessels may become overpressured because of an unbalanced reaction. Normally, sophisticated controls are used along with a safety valve in these cases.

- **Hydraulic expansion** - when a cold fluid is blocked in on hot exchanger surfaces, it will expand causing a rise in pressure.

- **Accumulation of noncondensables** - these do not accumulate

146

under normal conditions since they are released with the process streams; however, with certain piping configurations, it is possible for noncondensables to accumulate to the point that they may prevent condensation of a process stream in a condenser, thus resulting in overpressure.

In the case of uncontrolled fires, heat absorbed by exposed vessels or equipment causes vapor generation of the contents. A pressure relief valve is required to protect the vessel and relieve the generated vapor.

Each pressure relief valve should be individually analyzed for potential causes of overpressure. Valves should be sized for those situations that will require the maximum relieving rate. If a fire condition is controlling, two separate safety valves, one for a fire emergency and the other for an operational failure should be provided since the former is less likely to occur.

For fire emergencies an important consideration is the wetted surface area. The exposed surface area which is effective in generating vapor is that area wetted by its internal liquid level up to a maximum height of 25 ft above grade (this is the normal practice based on the average flame length). "Grade" is defined as any horizontal solid surface on which liquid could accumulate, i.e., roofs, solid platform, etc. The contents under variable level conditions would ordinarily be taken at the average inven-

tory. Liquid-full vessels, horizontal or vertical (such as trea-
ters), operate with no vapor space, and the wetted surface would
be the total vessel area to a maximum height of 25 ft. above
grade. It should be noted that, in such a vessel, at the start
of a fire the opening of the pressure relief may be due to
thermal expansion of the liquid. The valve should, however, be
sized based on the vapor generator at the relief pressure and the
boiling point corresponding to that pressure.

The surface areas of typical vessels used in process operations are as follows:

- **Surge and reflux drums:** The wetted surface should be
  calculated using the high liquid level or 50% of the
  total vessel surface, whichever is greater, since 50% is
  the normal liquid level in these vessels.

- **Knock-out drums:** - knock-out drums usually operate with
  low liquid levels. If the normal level is not known, the
  inventory at the high level alarm should be used to
  estimate the wetted surface area.

- **Fractionating columns:** - Fractionating columns usually
  operate with a normal liquid level in the bottom of the
  column plus a level on each tray. However, the entire
  wall of a fractionating column within the fire height
  limitation of 25 ft should be considered as wetted.

- **Working storage tanks:** - Here the liquid level is

independent of operation, and, therefore, the maximum level should be used for determining the wetted surface.

The wetted surface of spheres and spheroids are calculated as the area of the bottom half of the vessel or up to a height of 25 ft, whichever results in a greater surface area.

Where suitable drainage is provided to preclude an accumulation of flammable liquids directly beneath a vessel, the total heat input rate to the vessel may be computed from (as recommended by API publication RP 520):

$$Q = 21,000 \ FA^{0.82} \tag{1}$$

where
Q = total heat absorbed in Btu/hr

A = wetted surface in sq. ft

F = environmental factor

If insulation is required but the thickness is not known, an F-value of 0.3 is recommended. Figure 6-3 also provides a convenient plot of Equation 1 for graphical analysis.

If drainage is not provided for the area below the vessel (i.e., diked or curbed areas around a tank), then vapor relief for fire exposure should be computed from the following heat criteria:

- 20,000 Btu/hr/ft^2 for uninsulated vessel.

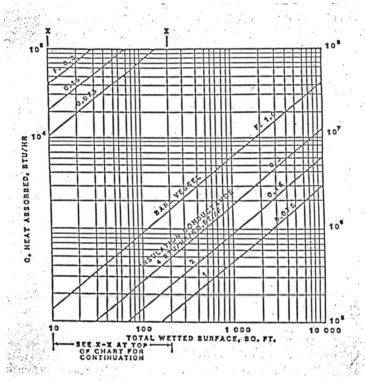

Figure 6-3. API formula for heat absorbed from fire on wetted surface of pressure vessel ($Q = 2,000$ $FA^{0.82}$). Source: API.

- 10,000 Btu/hr/ft^2 for 1 in. insulation.

- 6,000 Btu/hr/ft^2 for 2 in. insulation.

- 3,000 Btu/hr/ft^2 for 4 in. insulation.

These values are based on the wetted surface up to the normal liquid level, provided fireproof insulation is employed. With nonfireproof insulation it is best to assume that the vessel is bare.

For a fluid below the critical point (i.e., at relieving temperature and pressure), the vapor release rate can be computed from:

$$W = \frac{Q}{\lambda} \tag{2}$$

where W = vapor release rate lb/hr

Q = total heat input Btu/hr

λ = latent heat of fluid in vessel, evaluated relief valve inlet pressure Btu/lb.

No credit is normally taken for the sensible heat capacity of the fluid.

For a fluid above its critical point, i.e., when pressure relief conditions are near or above the critical point, the vapor discharge rate depends on the rate at which the fluid will expand. The latent heat of vaporization at or near the critical point is almost zero in this case.

151

Once relieving loads of individual pressure relief valves
are established, an analysis of the interactions between individual contributors is recommended. The simultaneous occurence of
two or more contingencies (i.e., double jeopardy) is highly
improbable and is therefore often neglected when establishing the
maximum system load. In detemining the maximum load from a
single contingency, all directly related contingencies which
influence the load must be considered. For example, in a plant
where a single boiler or source of steam is used for both process
drives and electric power generation, the failure of a steam
source (a single contingency) can cause simultaneous loss of
power (a directly related contingency). If the electric system
has an alternate source of supply, then only the loss of steam
need be considered, provided the elapsed time for transfer swit-
ching is not long enough to be ineffective. In this situation, a
power failure would not be a contingency directly related by the
loss of steam.

If a certain contingency were to involve more than one unit,
then the entire system must be evaluated. For example, if there
is more than one reaction vessel in series, then in the event of
a runaway reaction, all the reactors will be protected by a
single pressure relief valve. The same situation can occur in
the case of two or more fractionation columns in series. In the
case of multi-stage compressors having individual pressure relief

valves at each stage, the relieving rates from the pressure relief valves are not additive.

DESIGN METHODOLOGY FOR COLLECTION SYSTEMS

Vapors from different pressure relief valves and depressuring valves must first be collected in individual flare sub-headers located near each process area. Sub-headers must be interconnected to a main flare header which leads to a knock-out drum where condensates are removed. The number of main flare headers and individual sub-headers depends upon the type of vapors being handled as well as the temperature and the back pressure limitations of the pressure relief valves.

The pressure level of flare headers depends on the type of pressure relief valves employed and the pressure levels of the equipment connected to the flare system. The principal types of pressure relief valves are: conventional, balanced bellow type, piston type and pilot operated.

Conventional pressure relief valves are those where the disk of the valve is held tight against the inlet nozzle by means of a spring. Figure 5A illustrates a conventional safety relief valve normally used in refineries and chemical plants. This type of valve is least expensive, but it is limited by a back pressure of 10% of the maximum allowable working pressure. The reason for the limited back pressure is as follows: Assume P_1 to be the maximum allowable working pressure in the vessel. Since this is also the set pressure of the safety valve, the spring is so loaded that the total downward force on the valve disk is exactly equal to the total upward force exerted on it by the process vapor when it reaches pressure P_1. That is, the spring force F_s is related to the inlet nozzle area A_N through applied pressure P_1 ($F_s = P_1 A_N$). A slight pressure increase above P_1 lifts the valve disk up and releives the vapor through the discharge nozzle of the valve. Accumulation or overpressure above the maximum allowable working pressure (P_1) within the vessel is safe up to about 10% if the overpressure persists for a short period of time. Under normal operation when the operating pressure is below P_1, the downward force exerted by the spring on the disk exceeds the upward force exerted by the vapor. Hence, the disk is held tight against the inlet nozzle under normal operating conditions. When the back pressure exceeds atmospheric, the combined downward force exerted by the spring and the force developed due to the back pressure is $F_s + P_2 A_N$, where P_2 is the back pressure (see Figure 6-4A). In order to lift the valve disk against this combined downward force, the inlet vapor inside the vessel must be pressurized to a level greater than P_1. Hence, $P'_1 A_N = F_s + P_2 A_N$, where P'_1 is the new pressure developed.

Since the maximum pressure is $P'_1 = 1.1 P_1$,

$$UF_s = P_1 A_N$$

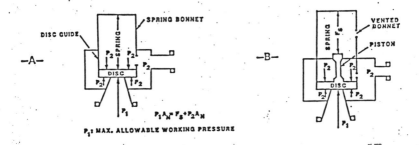

Figure 6-4. Shows effect of back pressure on (A) conventional safety valve; and (B) piston type valve.

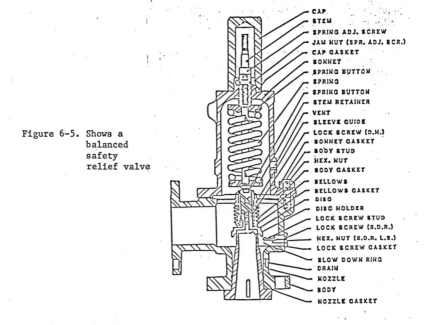

Figure 6-5. Shows a balanced safety relief valve

155

Hence

$$1.1P_1 \cdot A_N = P_1 A_N$$
$$P_2 = 0.1P_1$$

Thus, the maximum allowable back pressure is 10% of the maximum allowable working pressure of the vessel.

The remaining three types of pressure relief valves do not depend upon the back pressure for performance. However, to ensure that the safety valves work at their maximum capacity, the back pressure is limited to 50% of the relief valve set pressure. With the balanced bellows valve (see Figure 6.5), the spring does not act directly on the disk. Instead, it serves on a bellows first, which in turn acts on the disk. The piston type works in a similar fashion. The cross - sectional area of both the piston and the bellows is the same as the inlet nozzle of the valve. The effect of the back pressure on the top and the bottom of the disk creates equal balancing forces (i.e., $P_1 A_N$ equals F_s).

Pilot-operated valves combine a pilot valve with the main valve. The spring of the main valve provides 75% loading on the disk and the remaining 25% is offered by the gas or vapor through the pilot valve. When the vessel reaches the maximum allowable working pressure, the pilot valve relieves the gas pressure which contributes to the disk load. Thus the safety valve becomes wide open (see Figure 6-6).

156

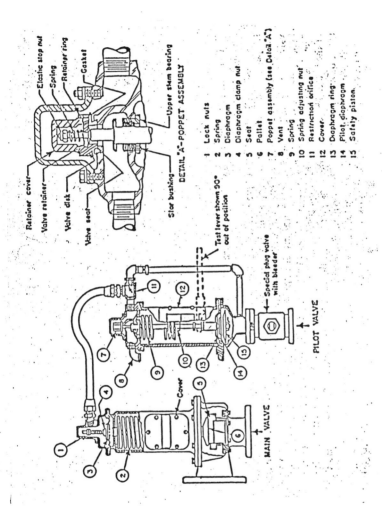

DETAIL "A"—POPPET ASSEMBLY

Retainer cover
Valve retainer
Valve disk
Valve seat
Stem bushing
Upper stem bearing
Gasket
Retainer ring
Spring
Elastic stop nut

1 Lock nuts
2 Spring
3 Diaphragm
4 Diaphragm clamp nut
5 Seat
6 Pallet
7 Poppet assembly (see Detail "A")
8 Vent
9 Spring
10 Spring adjusting nut
11 Restriction orifice
12 Cover
13 Diaphragm ring
14 Pilot diaphragm
15 Safety piston.

Test lever shown 90°
out of position

Special plug valve
with bleeder

PILOT VALVE

MAIN VALVE

Cover

Figure 6-6. Pilot operated safety valve.

157

With nonconventional valves, the maximum allowable back pressure should be taken as 50% of the valve set pressure. This limit approaches the critical flow pressure. If the back pressure exceeds the critical flow pressure corresponding to the set pressure of the safety valve, the total pressure drop available for flow decreases. This state can potentially lead to overpressurization. The recommended back pressure is, therefore, a maximum 40% to 50% of the set pressure.

The design pressure levels of process equipment connected to a flare system also establish flare header pressure levels. In some cases, pressure fluctuations are significant. Hence, it is not always economical to interconnect the entire process to a common header. It is often more economical to arrange for flare headers of two pressure levels, one connecting the low pressure system and the other connecting a high pressure system.

The basis for collecting philosophy of a flare system is based upon economics. A summary of the methodology is outlined below.

First consider the number of flare headers required. This depends on the economics, streamlined to accomodate minimum piping lengths and sizes. The following steps outline the procedure for comparative estimations:

- Study of the plot plan layout: From the plot plan layout the number of safety valves, set pressures, individual

relieving loads, relieving vapor temperatures, and properties of vapors must be noted.

- A single sub-header in each process area is drawn up
  connecting area pressure relief valves or depressuring
  valves.

- The sub-headers are then connected to provide a single
  main flare header based on the shortest route.

- The equivalent length of the main flare header is then
  calculated from the flare stack to the last safety valve,
  taking into consideration the straight length of the pipe
  and approximate equivalent lengths for bends, etc. If
  the actual location of the flare stack is not known a
  conservative estimate of 500 ft from the last piece of
  equipment can be assumed.

- A trial estimate of the diameter of the flare header
  based on the maximum relieving flare load and a back
  pressure limitation of 10% for conventional valves and
  40% for balanced type valves is made. Note, however, a
  single main header in most cases, turns out to be too
  large to be economical.

- A second trial is required for two main flare headers,
  one collecting the low pressure flares (usually 5 to 10
  psig), and the other collecting relatively high pressure
  flares (usually 15 to 20 psig). The two headers are

connected to their indivudual knock-out drums are combined into a single header which is connected to the
flare stack.

The maximum simultaneous load in each header must be
calculated separately and the pressure drop is to be
computed for the entire length of the pipe including the
combined length from the knock-out drum to the stack.

The sub-headers in each process area similarly will
have two levels of flare headers. The line sizing of
each level of sub-header in an individual area will
depend on the maximum simultaneous flow in that area.
Thus, the line sizing criterion of a sub-header may be
the largest single flow due to a blocked outlet condition. This flow may not necessarily be the controlling
load for the flare stack.

- The materials of construction determine the final number
of flare headers. Vapors that normally require expensive
materials are: corrosive vapors (e.g., SO_2, H_2S), high
temperature vapors (e.g., high temperature gases used for
regeneration of catalysts in reactors), and low temperature vapors (e.g., vapors generated due to flashing across a control valve or a safety valve in a cryogenic
system).

- Wet and dry flares - sometimes relatively hot vapors

carrying condensates may be separated from cold dry vapors. They do not run as separate headers, but either
low pressure or high pressure flare headers may be associated with any one of them. Thus, a wet flare header
may be, in fact, the low pressure header, and the dry
flare header may be the high pressure flare headers may
be associated with any one of them. Thus, a wet flare
header may be, in fact, the low pressure header, and the
dry flare header may be the high pressure flare or vice
versa.

- After the total number of flare headers has been established it may be necessary to recheck the vapor load in
  individual headers since introduction of a separate header may allow subtraction of the flow quantity from the
  low pressure header to which it was initially added.

Once the maximum vapor relieving requirement and the maximum
allowable back pressure have been established, line sizing is
performed with conventional calculations. The flare piping system can be divided into the following sections:

- Individual discharge lines from the pressure relief valves.

- The sub-headers in each area connecting the discharge
  lines.

- The main flare header (or headers) connecting the sub-headers leading to the knock-out drum(s).

- The final header connecting the vapor line(s) from the knock-out drum(s) leading to the flare stack.

Since vapors in the flare headers are relieved from a high pressure system to atmospheric, there is an appreciable kinetic energy change throughout the line. Since compressible flow e-xists in the flare headers and lines are reasonably long, isothe-rmal conditions may be assumed. When short well-insulated vapor lines are employed, adiabatic flow is a better approximation. In general, all vapor flows that normally occur in process plants are somewhere in between adiabatic and isothermal. It has been observed that for the same flow rate and pressure drop, line sizing calculations based on compressible isothermal conditions provide an equal or a larger diameter pipe, and therefore, flare headers should be sized based on the more conservative predic-tions derived from isothermal conditions. The following criteria are used in sizing flare headers:

- The back pressure developed at the downstream section of any pressure relief valve connected to the same headers should not exceed the allowable limit, i.e., 10% of the set pressure in psig for the conventional type and 40% to 50% of the set pressure in psig for the balanced type valve.

- Since the pressure drop is high, there is a possibility

of approaching sonic conditions. This results in a potential noise problem. It is a good practice to limit the
velocity to 60% of the sonic velocity or 0.6 Mach number.

The method of Lapple provides good line-sizing estimates.
The method employs a theoretical critical mass flow based on an
ideal nozzle at isothermal conditions. For a pure gas, the mass
flow can be computed from:

$$G_{ci} = 12.6P_0 \left(\frac{M}{(2Z-1)\, t_0} \right)^{0.5}$$

(3)

where G_{ci} = maximum mass flow or critical mass flow
($lb/sec/ft^2$).

P_0 = upstream pressure lb/in^2. abs.

M = molecular weight

T_0 = upstream temperature ($^\circ$R)

Z = compressibility factor

The actual mass flow, G ($lb/secft^2$) is a function of the
critical mass flow G_{ci}, the line resistance N, and the ratio of
the downstream to upstream pressures. These relationships are
plotted in Figure 8. In the area below the dashed line, the
ratio of G to G_{ci} remains constant, indicating that sonic flow
exists. Thus, in sizing flare headers the condition must lie
above the dashed line in Figure 6-7. The line resistance, N, is:

163

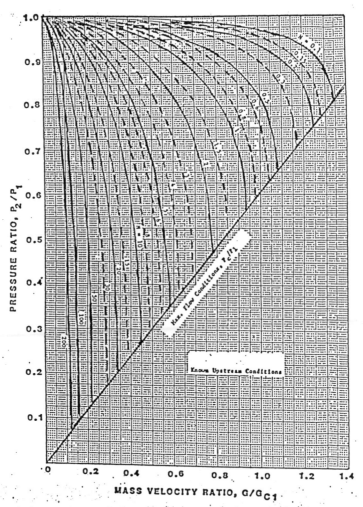

Figure 6-7. Pressure drop chart reported by Lapple.

$$N = \frac{4fL}{D} + \Sigma K_i \qquad\qquad (4)$$

where   L = equivalent length of line (ft)

         D = line diameter (ft)

         f = Fanning friction factor

         N = line resistance factor (dimensionless)

         K_i = resistance coefficients for pipe fittings (refer to table 6-1 for values) [Moody].

Lapple's method is useful when the upstream pressure of a header is known and the downstream pressure is to be evaluated. However, it is worthwhile to evaluate the pressure profile in the flare header as a function of distance from the stack. For this reason, one should calculate the pressure drop backwards, starting from the flare stack exit where the pressure is atmospheric. Figure 6-8 provides an alternate basis for evaluating pressure losses when the downstream pressure is known.

Although Figures 6-7 and 6-8 can be used for line sizing, it should be noted that the former requires more extensive trial and error.

The following steps summarizes the procedure for sizing flare headers:

     - The pressure at the base of the flare stack is approxi-

165

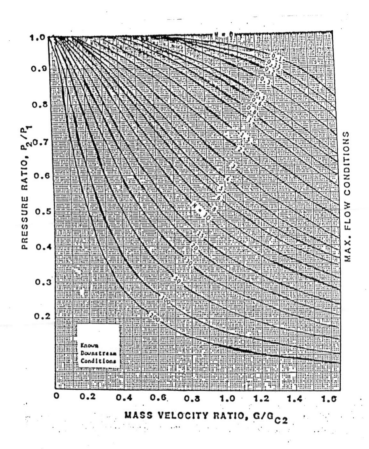

Figure 6-8. Pressure drop chart reported by Loeb.

mated as 2 psig. The pressure at the base may vary slightly depending on the type of seal used in the stack. Hence,

Pressure at the base = Atm. pressure at the flare exit + 0.5 psi at the flare tip

  P + 0.5 psi mol. seal P + 1 psi

  P due to flow through the stack height = 2 psig

- Compute the pressure in the knock-out drum:

  = 2 psig + P required for the flow of the full load vapors from the knock-out drum to the stack + 0.5 psi P assumed inside the knock-out drum.

- For an initial trial, an inside pipe diameter is assumed based on 60% of the sonic velocity corresponding to the pressure and temperature at the base of the stack, i.e., at 2 psig and temperature = T_0 (upstream temperature since isothermally is assumed).

167

The sonic velicity can be computed from:

$$V_s = 233 \frac{kT}{M} \qquad (5)$$

where

V_s = sonic velocity (ft/sec)

k = C_p/C_v of the gas normally between 1 to 1.8

T = temperature ($^\circ$R)

M = molecular weight

The flare load, W, (lbs/sec) is known. The density of the vapor at 2 psig, T_0 ($^\circ$R) is determined from the ideal gas law:

$$p = \frac{MP}{RT}$$

where

M = mol. wt.

P = pressure in psia

T = $^\circ$R

R = gas constant

Hence

$$\frac{4W}{\pi d^2} = \rho \times 223 \sqrt{\frac{\kappa T}{M}} \qquad (6)$$

where

d = pipe I.D. (ft)

The inside diameter d can then be computed from Equation 6.

Once the diameter is known the Reynolds number, R_e, can be computed and the friction factor f obtained from Figure 6-9.

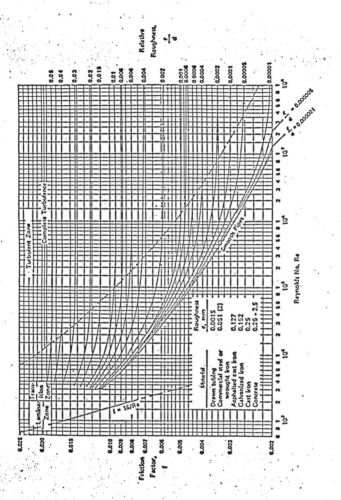

Figure 6-9.   Generalized Moody chart for obtaining friction factor.

Assuming a straight length of pipe for L = 500 ft, N (line resistance factor) can be calculated. Next G_{ci} is computed based on the downstream pressure and G/G_{c2} evaluated. From Figure 9 the ratio P_2/P_0 can be obtained. Since P_2 is known, p_0 can then be calculated. The pressure at the inlet of the knock-out drum is given by P_0 + 0.5 psi. Table 1 provides typical values of resistance coefficients for various pipe fittings.

- From the knock - out drum, the individual flare headers can be sized. Based on a Mach number of 0.6 and the density corresponding to (P_0 + 0.5) psia, a trial diameter can be established. The pressure at every intersection between the sub-header and the main header must be calculated, with the downstream pressure being (P_0 + 0.5)psia. Knowing the pressure at the intersection of the sub-header and the main header, the pressure at the intersection of the sub-header and the discharge pipe of the safety valve is computed. Usually the discharge pipe of the safety valve is small and hence, a separate pressure drop calculation is not necessary. However, the velocity at the discharge pipe should be checked to ensure that it is below sonic conditions. If the discharge pipe runs a considerable distance before it ties in with the sub-header, a separate pressure drop calculation will be needed.

170

TABLE 6-1.
Resistance Coefficient K for Various Pipe Fittings

Fitting	K	Fitting	K
Globe valve, open	9.7	90° double-miter elbow	0.59
Typical depressuring valve, open	8.5	Screwed tee through run	0.50
Angle valve, open	4.6	Fabricated tee through run	0.50
Swing check valve, open	2.3	Lateral through run	0.50
180° close screwed return	1.95	90° triple-miter elbow	0.46
Screwed or fabricated tee through branch	1.72	45° single-miter elbow	0.46
90° single-miter elbow	1.72	180° welding return	0.43
Welding tee through branch	1.37	45° screwed elbow	0.43
90° standard screwed elbow	0.93	Welding tee through run	0.38
60° single-miter elbow	0.93	90° welding elbow	0.32
45° lateral through branch	0.76	45° welding elbow	0.21
90° long-sweep elbow	0.59	Gate valve, open	0.21

d/d':	0	0.2	0.4	0.6	0.8
Contractions (USASI)	0	—	—	—	—
Contractions (sudden)	0.5	0.46	0.21	0.135	0.039
Enlargements (USASI)	—	—	0.38	0.29	0.12
Enlargements (sudden)	0.0	0.95	0.74	0.41	0.11

The sum of all the pressure losses starting from the flare stack up to the safety valve yields the total back pressure. This back pressure must be lower than the maximum back pressure allowed in the system and corresponding to the lowest set pressure of the safety valve.

DESIGN METHODOLOGY FOR CONDENSATE REMOVAL

Material entering the knock-out drum (or blow-down drum) will be a mixture of vapor and liquid. Liquid particle sizes less than 150 microns in size are readily burned in a flare, however, larger particles must be removed in the knock-out drum. This condensate is pumped out from the bottom of the knock-out drum either for reuse or disposal.

In some process plants (e.g., ethylene production, coal gasifaction plant) hot vapors containing water are collected in a separate flare header (called a wet flare header). Liquid collected in the knock-out drum for the wet flare contains water and liquid hydrocarbons. In the same manner cold and dry hydrocarbon vapors are collected in a dry flare header. The hydrocarbon liquid collected in the knock-out drum of the dry flare is usually vaporized in a vaporized located immediately below the knock-out drum and sent back to the flare. Figure 6-11A shows a dry flare knock-out drum with a vaporizer at the bottom.

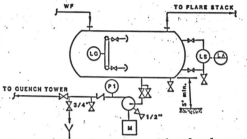

Figure 6-]0. Typical knock-out drum with a level gauge, level switch, and
level alarm.
Also shows a 2 inch utility connection for cleaning the drum
with steam and a pump-out pump with pressure indicator and
drum connection

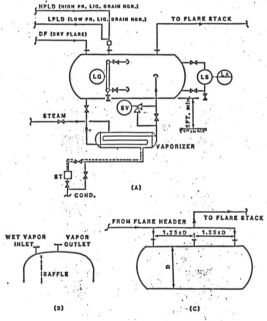

Figure 6-11. (A) Dry-flare knock-out drum. (B) shows vertical drum
arrangement; (C) althernative split feed arrangement
of knock-out drum.

173

Knock-out drums are either horizontal or vertical types. They are also available in a variety of configurations / arrangements that include:

- A horizontal drum with the vapor entering at one end of the vessel and exiting at the top of the opposite end (no internal baffling).
- A horizontal drum with vapor inlets at each end of the horizontal axis, and a center outlet.
- A horizontal drum with the vapor entering in the center and exiting at the two ends on the horizontal axis.
- A vertical drum with the vapor entering at the top. These are equipped with a baffle that directs the flow downward. The outlet nozzle is located at the top of the vertical axis (as shown in Figure 6-11B)
- A vertical drum with a tangential nozzle.

A split entry or exit reduces the drum size for large throughputs. As a rule of thumb, when the drum diameter exceeds 12 ft, the split flow arrangement is normally more economical. Figure 6-11C shows a split flow horizontal drum with the recommended dimensions.

Knock-out drums are usually sized by trial and error. Liquid particles drop out when the vapor velocity travelling through the drum is sufficiently low. In other words, the drum must be of sufficient diameter to effect the desired liquid-vapor separation.

Tan gives the following formula for sizing horizontal drums:

$$W = 360D^2 \sqrt{(p_L - p_G)\ MP/T}$$ (7)

where W = lb/hr of vapor

p_L = liquid density (lb/ft^3)

p_G = gas density (lb/ft^3)

M = mol. wt. of the vapor

T = temperature of the vapor ($^\circ$R)

P has units of psia, D in ft.

The formula is valid for particle sizes up to 400 microns.

Similar expressions are available for vertical knock-out drums. A formula for the vapor velocity is:

$$V_r = 0.4 \sqrt{\frac{p_L - p_G}{p_G}}\ (\text{ft/sec})$$ (8)

SEAL SYSTEMS

Standard practice is to provide a seal at the base of the flare to prevent flashbacks from occurring. In the absence of a seal, a continuous quantity of gas must be bled to the flare to maintain a net positive flow. Seals are of two main types: liquid and gas.

Liquid seals are further classified as seal drums and seal

pipes. In the former, a liquid seal is used in a seal drum located between the knock-out drum and the flare stack in place of a drum. This is often an integral part of the stack. Seal drums are either vertical or horizontal (see Figure 6-12A and 6-12B). The selection of the seal drum depends on the available space. Its purpose is to maintain a seal of several inches on the inlet flare header, preferably not exceeding 6 inches, other-wise it imposes back pressure to the knock-out drum. Water is normally used as a sealing liquid, and there is always a conti-nuous flow of water with the overflow going to the sewer. If located in a cold climate either the water must be heated by a submerged steam heater or alternately the water may be replaced by liquids such as as alcohol, kerosene, etc., which do not require continuous flow.

The capacity of the seal drum is usuallthe volume corres-ponding to 8 to 10 ft of the vapor inlet line. In a vertical drum, the ratio of the inlet pipe cross-sectional area to the vessel free area for gas flow above the liquid should be at least 1 to 3 to prevent gas flow surges to the flare. The area for the gas above the liquid interface should be at least equal to that of a circle having a diameter D equal to 2d, where d is the inlet gas pipe diameter. This is derived as follows:

Assuming a vertical vessel of cross-sectional area $(\pi/4)D^2$ and inlet pipe $(\pi/4)d^2$, the annular area is $(\pi/4)(D^2-d^2)$. Since

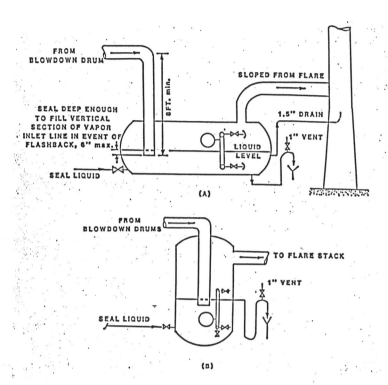

FROM
BLOWDOWN DRUM

SLOPED FROM FLARE

8 FT. min.

SEAL DEEP ENOUGH
TO FILL VERTICAL
SECTION OF VAPOR
INLET LINE IN EVENT OF
FLASHBACK, 6" max.

1.5" DRAIN

1" VENT

LIQUID
LEVEL

SEAL LIQUID

(A)

FROM
BLOWDOWN DRUMS

TO FLARE STACK

1" VENT

SEAL LIQUID

(B)

Figure 6-12. (A) Shows a horizontal seal drum; (B) a vertical seal drum.

the suggested ratio is 1:3, $D^2-d^2 = 3d^2$ or $D = 2d$.

The height of the vapor space above the liquid level in a vertical drum should be approximately 2 to 3 times the diameter (d) to provide disengaging space for entrained seal liquid. If a horizontal seal vessel is used, a minimum dimension of 3 ft between liquid level and top of the drum is recommended.

Seal pipes located at the base of the stack are less costly than drums. However, they can experience flow pulsations at low throughputs. Also, during large gas releases, the water seal may be blown out of the top to the flare stack. Some general guidelines for sizing seal legs are as follows:

The slope of the inlet line is designed to provide a volume of water below the normal sealing water level equivalent to a volume of 10 ft of the inlet pipe.

The depth of the water seal should not exceed 12 inches to prevent gas pulsation.

- The seal water level is maintained by a continuous flow of water at about 20 gallons per minute.

- Normal overflow is taken off the bottom of the seal leg. The height of the seal leg should be equivalent to about 175% of the pressure at the base of the stack during maximum vapor release so that gas release at the base is prevented. Figure 6-13 illustrates a typical seal leg arrangement.

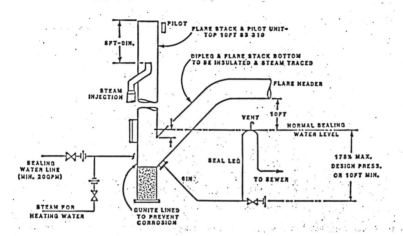

Figure 6-13. Seal-leg arrangement. Source: Perry.

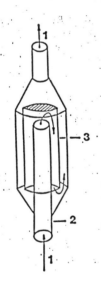

Figure 6-14. Shows a molecular seal. Note that the molecular seal is flange-connected to the burner tip at the top and to flare stack section at the bottom: (1) flare gas (intermittent flow) and purge gas (continuous); (2) main section (having same diameter as stack) (3) inverted bucket.

179

An alternate gas seal is the "molecular" type seal which employs a purge gas having a molecular weight of 28 or less (e.g., N_2, CH_4, or natural gas). Because of the buoyancy of the purge gas, a zone having a pressure exceeding atmospheric is created. The molecular seal is located at the top of the flare stack immediately before the burner tip. Ambient air cannot enter the stack because of this high pressure. The recommended purge velocity through the molecular seal is about 0.1 ft/sec. If a molecular seal is not used, the recommended velocity is 1 ft/sec, thereby increasing the purge gas requirement. Figure 16 shows the features of the molecular seal.

FLARE BURNERS

Flare burners are located at the tip of the flare stack, with the top section typically about 12 ft in length. The burner diameter is sized to accomodate a specified velocity. Flame blow-out occurs when the exit velocity of vapors exceeds 20 to 30 percent sonic conditions (Tam).

It is therefore good practice to size burners to accommodate discharge velocities less than 20 percent of the sonic velocity. The mass flow rate through the burner is:

$$W = 3,600 \ p_G A_c \qquad (9)$$

where   W = mass flow rate (lb/hr)

p_G = density of the gas (lb/ft^3)

A_c = cross-sectional area (sqft)

The vapor density is:

$$p_G = \frac{MP}{10.73T}$$

and since the exit velocity equals 20 percent of sonic:

$$V = \frac{1}{5}\sqrt{\frac{g_c \kappa RT}{M}} \qquad (10)$$

Hence, the flare tip cross-section is:

$$A_c = \frac{0.785}{144} = d^2 \qquad (11)$$

where M = molecular weight
P = absolute pressure of vapor (psia)
T = temperature (°F)
g_c = conversion factor, $32.17 \frac{(lb_m)\,(ft)}{lb_f(sec^2)}$
R = gas constant, $1,546 \frac{(ft-lb_f)}{(°R)\,(mole)}$
$\kappa = C_p/C_v = 1.2$ assumed
d = diameter of flare tip (in.)

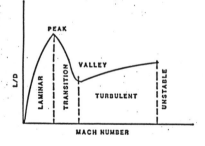

Figure 6-15. Burning characteristics of flames from circular ducts discharging vertically into quiescent air without premixing.

Combining the above equations and using the value for $g_c, k,$ R, and P   (whereP = 14.7 psia):

$$d^2 = \frac{W}{1,370}\sqrt{\frac{T}{M}} \qquad\qquad (12)$$

If based on the maximum rate, the diameter will be too large, then the normal flow must be used and checked for 40% of sonic velocity for the maximum load.

SAFETY CONSIDERATIONS FOR FLARING

The location of a flare stack is a safety related issue. Normally, it is located in areas which are on the leeward side of the plant (downstream of prevailing winds) and remote from operating and trafficked zones.

The height of the flare stack depends on several factors, namely:

- Heat released by the flare gas.
- Characteristics of the flame and the flame length.
- Emissivity of the flame.
- Radiation intensity of the flame.
- Ground level concentration of toxic gases present in the flare stream in the event of a flame blowout.

The burning characteristics of flames and the flame length

are important parameters in sizing stacks. Burning characteristics are illustrated by the plots shown in Figures 6-15. through 6-17. The plot shows different zones of the flame spectrum in terms of dimensionless numbers which enables estimates of the critical flame points in each combustion zone. This helps to visualize how a flame profile may be superimposed on the loci of Figure 6-16.

Note that the flame height increases appreciably when combustible gas flow is sufficiently reduced so as to cause a shift into the laminar zone. By designing a flare tip which induces premixing of gas and air or selecting a "smokeless" design which induces partial premixing by agitation with steam, the increased peaking of the flare in the laminar zone may be avoided or reduced. This type of flare tip design also reduces the noise level.

Figure 6-14 should be used along with the following criteria:

- Peak at Reynolds number = 3,000
- Valley at Reynolds number = 5,000
- Blow off at Mach number = 0.2.

Note that the Reynolds number is based on the stack diameter. Each of the above criteria refers to the gas state prior to combustion at the exit from the stack tip. A Reynolds number of 3,000 applies to the "peak loci curve," a Reynolds number of

183

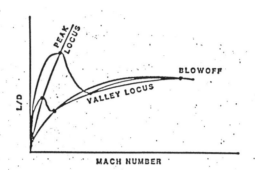

Figure 6-16. Shows superposition of typical flame characteristic on the locus curves

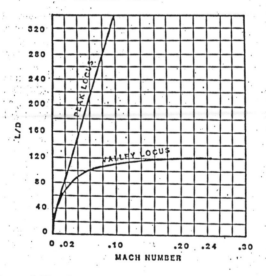

Figure 6-17. Plot of aspect ratio (L/D) versus Mach number.

5,000 applies to the "valley loci curve," and the blowoff mach number applies to the limit of the "valley loci curve". The blowoff point is reached when the velocity of gas leaving the stack causes the flame to separate from the tip at which point the flame becomes unstable.

For maximum stack discharge, a Mach number of 0.2 is recommended. From Figure 6-17 then, the corresponding L/D ratio is 118. From the stack diameter D, the flame length L can be determined.

The thermal radiation and escape time can be estimated from the data given in Table 6-2. Values are based on experimental data on the threshold limit of pain to the human body as a function of the radiation intensity in $Btu/hr/ft^2$, generated by a flame.

Figure6-18 is a plot of the data reported in Table 6-1. A safe level of heat radiation intensity for unlimited time exposure has been found to be 440 $Btu/hr/ft^2$. It is apparent that a time interval with varying radiation intensity must be allowed, to permit a human to escape from a suddenly released intense heat source. The varying radiation intensity results from an individual increasing his distance from the source of heat.

Assume an individual to be at the base of a flare stack when heat is suddenly being released. The average reaction time of an individual is between 3 to 5 seconds. Hence, during this short

TABLE 6-2.
Heat Radiation and Escape Time

Radiation Intensity (Btu/hr/ft²)	Time to Pain Threshold (seconds)
440	Infinite
550	60
740	40
920	30
1,500	16
2,200	9
3,000	6
3,700	4
6,300	2

From American Petroleum Institute

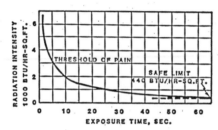

Figure 6-18. Plot of heat radiation vs exposure time for bare skin at the threshold of pain.

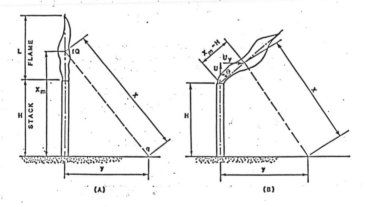

Figure 6-19. (A) Illustrates a flare stack and flame in stagnant surroundings; (B) shows flame in wind-blown environment.

reaction time interval, the full radiated heat intensity will be absorbed. Then follows another short time interval (20 ft/sec is normally assumed to be the average escape velocity of a man) during which continually decreasing amounts of heat will be absorbed until a safe distance is reached (heat intensity for a safe location is 440 Btu/hr/sq.ft. and lower from Figure 6-15).

The maximum heat intensity which may be tolerated at the base of the stack corresponding to the limiting total heat absorbed may then be determined by

$$t_a \cdot q_a = t_r q_m + t_e \frac{q_M - q_m}{\ln \frac{(q_M)}{(q_m)}} \qquad (13)$$

where $\quad t_a = t_r + t_e$ (total time exposed = reaction time + escape time)

$t_a q_a \quad = \quad$ total heat flow/area for the exposure time

$q_M \quad = \quad$ maximum radiation intensity

$q_m \quad = \quad$ minimum radiation intensity

Figure 6-18 is the solution of the preceding equation. The escape time interval t_e depends on the stack height H. Therefore, the use of Figure 6-18 will not be fully understood until stack height criteria are established.

The following steps outline the approach to determine the flare stack height based on the radiation intensity:

187

- Calculate the radiation intensity using the following equation:

$$q = \frac{\varepsilon' Q}{4\pi X^2} \tag{14}$$

where
q = radiation intensity (Btu/hr/sqft).

ε' = emissivity of the flame

Q = heat generated by the flame (Btu/hr)

X = distance from the center of flame, X_m feet above grade to point (ft) (refer to Figure 6-19A)

Flame emissivity values for common gases are as follows (Kent):

Gas	ε'
Hydrocarbon	0.4
Propane	0.33
Methane	0.2

A relationship between ε' and the net calorific value of a gas can be used in the absence of data [11]:

$$\varepsilon' = 0.2 \left(\frac{h_c}{900} \right) 1/2 \tag{15}$$

where
h_c = net heat value of a gas (NHV) in Btu/scf (60° F, 14.7 psia)

- Calculate the heat flow Q, Btu/hr

188

$$Q = Wh_c \frac{379}{M} \qquad \qquad (16)$$

where W = lb/hr of vapors released

             h_c = net heating value of gas in Btu/scf (60° F, 14.7

                psia)

            M = molecular weight of the gas

The formula for the stack height is first derived. Referring to Figure 6-19

where $X^2 = X_m^2 + y^2$

           $X_m = \sqrt{H(H+L)}$

where X_m = distance of the point of maximum intensity from grade (ft)
           H = stack height (ft)
           L = flame length (ft), L is 118D as shown

Hence

$X^2 = H(H+L) + y^2$

And from Equation 14

$$q_M = \frac{\varepsilon' Q}{4\pi H(H+L)}$$

where q_M is the maximum radiation intensity at the base of the flare (i.e., at y = 0 or x = X_m).

Hence, H is derived as:

$$H = \frac{1}{2}\left[\left(L^2 + \frac{\varepsilon' Q}{\pi q_m}\right)^{1/2} - L\right] \qquad \qquad (17)$$

The shortest stack is obtained when q_M = 3,300 Btu/hr/sqft or from Figure 22 at t_e = 0. The limiting safe radial distance from the flame is:

$$X = \left[\frac{\varepsilon' Q}{4\pi 440}\right]^{1/2} \quad \text{and} \quad X^2 = \frac{\varepsilon' Q}{5,530}$$

Note that y = radial distance from the base of the stack = $[X^2 - H(H+L)]^{1/2}$. Allowing for the speed of escape (20 ft/sec) we have:

$$y = 20t_e = [X^2 - H(H+L)]^{1/2} \qquad \qquad (18)$$

This defines the safety boundary, corresponding to quiescent ambient air.

Thus the stack height H, the limiting heat radiation q_m, and the radial distance; y, can be evaluated by a trial and error procedure by assuming a value of t_e.

The above analysis mut be extended to account for the more prevalent case of wind circulation in the vicinity of the flare. For locations where wind intensity is unknown, it is suggested that an average 20 mph wind be assumed acting in all directions which results in increasing the safe circular boundary by the resulting tilt of the flame. (This is illustrated in Figure 21B). The flame tilt and its effect on the safety boundary increase may be determined as follows:

$$\tan \theta = \frac{U_w}{U}$$

where

U_w = wind velocity

U = flare exit velocity

U_w = $(X_m - H) \sin \theta$

U_t = $(X_m - H) \cos \theta$

y = $\{X^2 - (H+(X_m-H)\cos\theta)^2\}^{1/2} + (X_m-H)\sin \theta$ (19)

This formula establishes the limiting boundary for wind circulation. When evaluating wind effects on flame tilt, an average wind intensity should be used in the calculations.

The preceding analysis leads to a conservative design since calculations are based on thermal effects to bare skin. If protective clothing is worn by operating personnel along with proper shielding to reduce heat radiation, the required stack height can be greatly reduced. There is however, a tradeoff in that the safety boundary increases. Since the head load of the flare, the flame length, and the safe radiation intensity (440 Btu/hr/sqft) remain the same, decreasing the stack height leads to an increase in the safety envelope.

An alternative method of stack height sizing is based on the allowable limit for radiation intensity. For operating personnel, the allowable intensity is 1,500 Btu/hr/sqft and for equipment 3,000 Btu/hr/sqft.

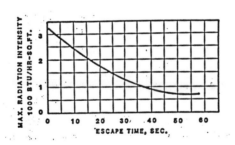

Figure 6-20. Plot of maximum radiation intensity vs. escape time, assuming a five-second reaction time.

The 1,500 Btu/hr/ft-1R2 criterion is based on the following. In emergency releases, a reaction time of an operation 3 to 5 seconds may be assumed. Perhaps 5 to 10 seconds more would elapse before the average individual could escape the area with an average escape velocity of 20 ft/sec. This would result in a total exposure period ranging from 8 to 15 seconds. The time to pain threshold corresponding to 1,500 Btu/hr/ft^2 is 16 seconds (from Table 6-1), before the individual could escape to a safe place. The effect of heat radiation on equipment is shown in Figure 6-21. The temperature of metal equipment increases with exposure time and the higher the radiant heat intensity, the greater the temperature. Curve 1 in Figure 6-22 shows the theoretical equilibrium temperatures based on a view factor of 0.5. The actual temperature on surfaces facing the flame will lie between curves 1 and 2.

The temperature of vessels containing liquid or flowing vapors may be lower because of cooling effects. Curve 2 applies to materials having a low heat conductivity coefficient (e.g., wood). In this case, equilibrium temperatures are reached within a shorter time as compared with metal objects. Dehydration of wood takes place at about 500° F, decomposition at 700° F, and ignition at around 800° F, corresponding to 1,300, 3,000. and 4,000 Btu/hr/ft^2, respectively. This means that wooden structures and vegetation exposed to heat intensities of 3,000 to

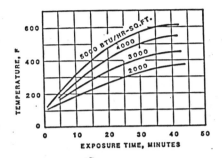

Figure 6-21. Plot of temp. of steel equipment vs. exposure time for different radiant heat intensities. Curves are based on 1/4 inch plate thickness with an effective emissivity of 10 and view factor of 0.5. Cooling caused by convection, etc., is neglected.

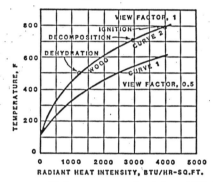

Figure 6-22. Plot of equilibrium temperature vs. radiant heat intensity: Curve 1-metal equipment Curve 2- wood.

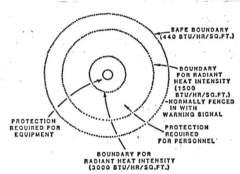

Figure 6-23. Shows circles of radiant heat intensity.

193

4,000 Btu/hr/ft^2 and higher may catch fire and burn. Paint on equipment may also be damaged. Therefore, it is recommended that equipment located in this area be protected by proper heat shielding or emergency water sprays.

The following steps outline design calculations by the alternate method:

- Compute the radial distance from the flame using Equation 14 for q = 15,000 Btu/hr/sqft.
- Compute the safe radial distance at q = 440 Btu/hr/sqft (Equation 14).
- A suitable value for q is assumed at the base of the stack. q = 3,000 Btu/hr/sqft is a good start since protective shielding will be provided at the stack.
- From Equation 17 compute H.

Figure 6-23 illustrates the different heat intensity loci that should be examined.

After the stack height has been established from radiation intensity values, the maximum permissible ground level concentrations of toxic gases in the event of a flame blowout should be evaluated. Table 6-3 provides data on toxicologists threshold limits as reported by the Environmental Protection Agency (EPA).

Estimated ground level concentrations should be based on the emergency condition of a flame blowout. Calculations should be performed for a range of climatological conditions at the plant

194

TABLE 6-3.
Threshold Limits for Certain Toxic Substances Gases and Vapors

Gas or Vapor	PPM	Gas or Vapor	PPM
Acetaldehyde	200	Hydrogen solenie	0.05
Acetic acid	10	Hydrogen sulfide	20
Acetic anhydride	5	Isodine	0.1
Acetone	1,000	Isophorene	25
Acrolein	0.5	Isopropylamine	5
Acrylonitire	20	Mesityl oxide	50
Ammonia	100	Methyl acetate	200
Amyl acetate	200	Methyl acetylene	1,000
Amyl alcohol	100	Methyl alcohol	200
Aniline	5	Methyl bromide	20
Arsinic	0.05	2-Methoxyethanol	25
Benzene	35	Methyl chloride	100
Benzyl chloride	1	Methylcyclohexane	500
Bromide	1	Methylcyclohexanol	100
Butadiene	1,000	Methylcyclohexanone	100
Butyl alcohol	100	Methyl formate	100
Butylamine	5	Methyl amyl alcohol	25
Carbon dioxide	5,000	Methylene chloride	
Carbon disulfide	20	(dichloromethane)	500
Carbon monoxide	100	Naptha (coal tar)	200
Carbon tetrachloride	25	Naptha (petroleum)	500
Chlorine	1	pNitroaniline	1
Chlorobenzene	75	Nickel carbonyl	0.001
Chloroform	100	Nitrobenzene	1
Cresol (all isomers)	5	Nitroethane	100
Cyclohexane	400	Nitrogen dioxide	5
Cyclohezanol	100	Nitromethane	100
Cyclohexanone	100	Nitrotoluene	5
Cyclohexene	400	Octane	500
Cyclopropane	400	Ozone	0.1
Diacetone alcohol	50	Pentane	1,000
0-Dichlorobenzene	50	Propyl ketone	200
1,1-Dichloroethane	100	Phenol	5
Diethylamine	25	Phenylhydrazine	5
Diisobutyl ketone	50	Phosgene (carbonyl chloride)	1
Dimethylaniline	5	Phosphine	0.05
Dimethylsulfate	1	Phosphorus trichloride	0.5
Diethylene dioxide	100	Propyl acetate	200
Ethyl acetate	400	Propyl alcohol	400
Ethyl alcohol (ethanol)	1,000	Propyl ether	500
Ethylamine	25	Propylene dichloride	75
Ethylbenzene	200	Pyridine	10
Ethyl bromide	200	Quinone	0.1
Ethyl chloride	1,000	Stibine	0.1
Ethyl ether	400	Styrene	200
Ethylene chlorohydrin	5	Sulphur dioxide	10
Ethylenedriamine	10	Sulphur hexafluoride	1,000
Ethylene dibromide	25	Sulphur monochloride	1
Ethylene dichloride	100	Sulphur pentafluoride	0.025
Ethylene oxide	100	1,1,2,2-Tetrachloroethane	5
Fluorine	0.1	Tetranitromethane	1
Formaldehyde	5	Toluene (toluol)	200
Gasoline	500	o-Toluidine	5
Hydrazine	1	Trichloroethylene	200
Hydrogen bromide	5	Trichloroethane	500

site. For a rough estimate the following empirical formula (API) can be used.

$$C_{max} = \frac{3,697 \ vM \ \sigma z}{u \ H^2 \ \sigma y}$$

$$X_{max} = (H/\sigma z)^{2/2-N} \tag{20}$$

where   C = concentrationat grade in ppm (volume)

          v = specific volume of toxic gas (ft^3/lb)

          M = weight discharge of pollutant component (ton/day)

         σz = vertical diffusion coefficient

          u = air velocity at grade

          H = stack height (ft)

         σy = horizontal diffusion coefficient

       X_{max}= distance from stack to the point of maximum conc.(ft)

          N = Environmental factor

The following values are taken from the API Manual:

    σz = 0.13

    σy = 0.13

    N   = 0.25

Cheremisinoff et al. give detailed procedure for estimating pollution levels.

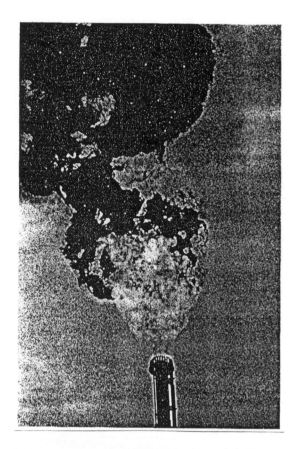

Figure 6-24. Low combustion efficiency results when unsaturated hydrocarbons are flared without using some system of enhancing mixing.

NOTATION

A	cross-sectional area	N	line resistance or environmental factor
$C_{p,v}$	specific heats at constant pressure and volume, respectively	P	pressure
C	concentration	Q	heat flow rate
d, D	diameter	q	heat flow per unit area
F	environmental factor	R	universal gas law constant
f	friction factor	Re	Reynolds number
G	mass flow rate per unit area	T	absolute temperature
g	gravitational acceleration	t	time
g_c	conversion factor	U	flare exit velocity
H	stack height	U_w	wind speed
h_o	heating value	V	velocity
K_i	resistance coefficient	W	vapor mass rate
L	length	X	distance from flame source
M	molecular weight	y	radial distance
Ma	Mach number	Z	compressibility factor

Greek Symbols

ε'	emmisivity	ν	specific volume
θ	angle	σ_y, σ_z	horizontal and vertical diffusion coefficients
κ	ratio of specific heats		
μ	viscosity		

REFERENCES

American petroleum Institute, **"Refinery Practice,"** 520: 8 (1969).

American petroleum Institute, **"Refinery Practice,"** 520 (Part I): 18 (1973).

American petroleum Institute, **"Refinery Practice,"** 520 (Part I): 26 (1973).

American petroleum Institute, **"Refinery Practice,"** 521: 45 (1969).

American petroleum Institute, **"Refinery Practice,"** 521: 50 (1969).

American petroleum Institute, **"Refinery Practice,"** 521: 35 (1969).

American petroleum Institute, **"Refinery Practice,"** 520: 64 (1969).

American petroleum Institute, **"Disposal of Refinery Wastes,"** 2:53 (1976) Ch 9.

Cheremisinoff, P.N., and Young, R.A., **"Pollution Engineering Practice Handbook,"** Ann Arbor Science Pub., Ann Arbor, MI (1976).

Cheremisinoff, P.N., and Young, R.A., (Eds.) **"Air Pollution Control and Design Handbook,"** Part I, Marcel Dekker Inc., NY (1977).

Kent, G.B., **"Practical Design of Flare Stacks,"** in Waste Treatment and Flare Stack Design Handbook, Hydrocarbon Processing, Texas, (1968).

Lapple, C.E., **"Trans. AIChE,"** 39: 385 (1943).

Loeb, M.B., Report Tr-256-D, John F. Kennedy Space Center (1965).

Moody, L.F., **"Trans. ASM E66,"** (1944).

Perry, R., Cecil, H., and Chilton, H., (Eds.) **"Chemical Engineers Handbook,"** 5th ed., McGraw - Hill Book Co., NY, 1972.

Tan, S.H., **"Flare Design Simplified,"** in Waste Treatment Flare Stack Design Handbook, Hydrocarbon Processing, Houston (1968).

INDEX

acid gas emissions 64
acid rain 64
adhesion 55
adiabatic flame 40
agglomeration 54
agitation 24
air 31, 98
air pollution 38
air ports 103
air requirement 14, 16
air starved 72
analytical requirement 130
arch height 94
auxiliary heat 99

back pressure 155, 156, 162
baffled chambers 56
batch burning 5
block valve 145
boiler 62, 65
Brownian motion 52
burners 75
burning 25
burning rate 102

calcination 116
catalytic incinerators 82
chemical process industry 72
chemical properties 105
chlorine 66
coagulation 54
combustible materials 30
combustion 1, 38
combustion air 98
combustion air ports 75
combustion calculations 21, 102
combustion equations 29
combustion product 8, 13, 20
compositions of refuse 7
condensate removal 172
controlled air 129
cooling 77
crossfeed beds 4, 13
Cunningham correction factors 50
curtain-wall 97

design 91
design calculations 102
design requirements 127
dimensional calculations 102
dioxin 63
doors 109
draft 101
draft velocities 103
drag coefficients 48, 51
drag coefficients for a sphere
drying 22, 24
Dulont formula 15
dust particles 56

electric reactors 121
elevated flare system 139
enthalpy 19, 20
entrained water 77
excess air 14, 16, 32, 35
exhaust fan 107

filtration 56
fires 147
firetube boilers 88
flame characteristic 184
flame port 97
flare burners 180
flare gas control 137
flare gas system 141
flare headers 162
flare tip 181
flares 82
flue gas 33, 34, 64
fluidized bed 6, 78, 116, 136
fossil fuels 38
fractionating columns 148
friction factor 169
frictional drag 49
fuel 5, 41
fuel value 43
fuel-to-air-ratio 3
furnace temperature 37

201